Kidding Around Town

Cool Places to Grow Smart Brains

by Catherine Cates, "The Around Town Mom"

DFW Edition

Kidding Around Town – Dallas/Fort Worth Edition

Copyright © 2014 by Catherine Cates

Mary Beth Smith
Park Cities Publishing
3032 Mockingbird Lane
Dallas, TX 75205

Ordering Information:

Quantity sales. Special discounts are available on quantity purchases by corporations, associations, and others. For details, contact the publisher at the address above.

Printed in the United States of America

This book is not intended to include all currently available locations in Dallas Fort Worth. For locations outlined in this edition of Kidding Around Town, all information provided within these pages is current at time of publication. Before venturing out, we recommend you check with each location to become familiar with any changes or modifications to existing or new exhibits and verify administrative information reflects the current status.

Table of Contents

Foreword

Catherine Cates and I have many things in common and not the least of which is our ability to create out of necessity. Independently we have contributed to a greater understanding of wonderful places and popular activities to advance learning for children and their families. My contribution, the *Outings and Adventures* series, was introduced to the Dallas/Ft Worth metroplex in 1997 and Catherine's contribution is seen in her website AroundTownKids.com, first developed in 2004.

That same year, we met at a Frisco parenting group where I was presenting information about infant and adolescent brain development and we instantly became friends. With our shared belief in the importance of growing smart kids and strong families, we started exploring north Texas together and discovered fun, interesting activities with our children.

As my children matured and began experiencing college, Catherine approached me with the idea of partnership. This idea has resulted in a new resource for parents to enjoy and it is in your hands.

I applaud Catherine and what she has done with my original pages. She has kept alive a wonderful and valuable resource every parent and adult with children should own. Her unique perspective rooted in her technical talents and business suave has opened the door to special features including expanded territory, a dollar-guide, map, and list of festivals.

So, grab your sneakers, a smart phone, and hop into your SUV; your adventure starts now!

Lynda Morley
Cultural Anthropologist
Author of the Outings and Adventures *series*

Preface

Welcome to Kidding Around Town.

I am pleased to announce the updated version of Lynda Morley's *Outings and Adventures* series. Let me introduce myself and how I came to this project.

In 2003, after my son was born, I joined a MOMS Club, a non-profit organization designed to support moms with young children in a social environment. I found this to be a rewarding part of my parenting life because it gave me an opportunity to use some of my professional skills while being with my young son.

By 2004, I was serving as president of the club. My responsibilities included planning monthly activities for members and their children. Very quickly I realized how difficult this was because I was unaware of the variety of activities Dallas-Fort Worth had to offer. The lack of centralized information made this task time consuming. It was because of this challenge that I created the first website to support the north Texas area, AroundTownKids.com.

Having been in the corporate world for over fifteen years, I yearned for my own business. My website, AroundTownKids.com, inspired by my own needs, is a kids' event calendar plus an online parent resource guide for camps, birthday parties and more providing information in an easy-to-find searchable format. Using the AroundTownKids app, parents can quickly discover places to go in the DFW metroplex.

Later this same year, I heard Lynda Morley, author of the *Outings and Adventures* series, speak at a parenting group. Her simple message encouraging parents and children to explore nearby locations to build strong brains and bonds, along with her energetic and passionate presentation style, motivated me and many others to purchase her book on the spot! Her words made me recognize that I, too, believed that, as parents, we are all teachers to our children. Without formal degrees, we practice the methods used by educators every time we impart information to our charges. I was thrilled to use my website, AroundTownKids. com, as a vital tool to practice what Morley endorsed, and in doing so I began to view these adventures as an important part of my son's development.

Over the next few years, Morley and I developed a friendship and went on many outings together. She taught me the basic principles involved to effectively exchange information between an adult and child, tools to use, and specific places to go. We have great fun together discovering quirky, interesting places with my son and her growing children.

Now, with her children experiencing life as young adults, Morley is focused on the adult brain leaving me with an opportunity to consult with her as I continue the *Outings and Adventures* series with my own version re-titled *Kidding Around Town*. This newest edition includes 189 locations to explore in Dallas Fort Worth, 34 location reviews, handy reference map, a Dollar Rating Guide and a list of DFW Festivals.

Catherine Cates
The Around-Town Mom
2014

Introduction:

Family Activities & Their Neurological Significance

This book is about the importance of families spending time together, exploring the world they live in, and the amazing neurological benefits of those discoveries. These benefits, first introduced to Dallas/Ft Worth parents in 1997 with the first edition titled, *Let's Go! A Guide to Outings and Adventures in Dallas/Ft Worth for Children Ages 1-5* and the subsequent editions in the *Outings and Adventures* series by by Lynda Morley, are further established in this resource with additional locations and activities around North Texas.

Kids whose families share time together grow to be well-adjusted, compassionate adults. Often the activities families share involve opportunities to explore and gather information about particular topics or concepts. This exploration and information gathering manifests itself in the creation of *dendrites*, which are vital to healthy brain development.

So what is a *dendrite*? A single dendrite is a neuron with extensions on both ends that look similar to tree branches. The tree branch extensions are used to attach to other neurons that develop as a result of like-stimulation. The brain identifies like-stimulations with a code and the brain recognizes approximately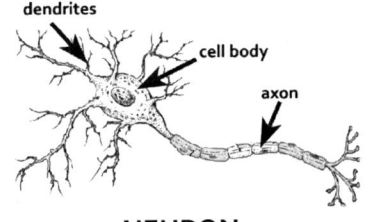

NEURON

100 unique codes. With repeated stimulation, the brain creates and stores a mass of uniquely coded dendrites which give the individual a greater propensity to understand and perform at advanced levels.

For example, when a two-year-old is introduced to simple arithmetic, the brain is stimulated to produce several thousand "math" dendrites. With repeated activities over the next couple years (including counting beyond 1-2-3, using manipulatives, working puzzles, and playing dice games), her brain creates a massive network of "math" dendrites. This large network forms a foundation for her to understand complex math concepts which, if pursued, will enable her to advance ahead of others. Conversely, a child who is not exposed to simple arithmetic activities until age five or six will be not be able to advance at the same rate as the child with earlier practice because his brain has only started to "learn" what the other child learned a couple years earlier.

Although space in this book does not allow for a more in-depth discussion on dendrite development and related brain functions such as pruning, social-emotional learning, and plasticity, these neurological happenings are connected to the way an individual retains information. Retaining information, or learning, involves experiencing many different types of activities and this book offers over 180 locations with specific activities designed to encourage development of a variety of coded dendrites while sharing time together.

Outdoor activities including nature hikes, environmental projects, and playgrounds require physical agility to aid mastery of positive self-esteem and balance. Art exhibits offer stimulation through a wide variety of styles, artists, mediums resulting in emotional connections that invoke feelings and thoughts. Live action and other theatre-based programs allow enhanced visual creativity, writing, language formation, and other oratory skills. Visiting museums and special exhibits increase development of critical thinking skills and processes while exploring new customs, life skill concepts and contemporary values.

We, Catherine Cates and Lynda Morley, invite you to expose your child (and yourself!) to the many diverse opportunities to grow strong brains while enjoying time together in a meaningful and purposeful way.

Catherine Cates
Lynda Morley

Kidding Around Town

Acknowledgments

Writing a book requires a team. I would like to thank my team for all their help, trust and support during this process. You have made writing this book much easier and for that I am grateful.

My most heartfelt thank you goes to Lynda Morley for her generous guidance, time and support as we transitioned this project. Our outings together have been so much fun they don't even seem like work!

Thank you to my son. Without him I would not have been inspired to start my business or work on this book. Because of him I have been able to put my educational outing skills to use.

Thank you to my husband for going on outings with us and for his continued support as he always believes in me.

Thank you to my publisher, Mary Beth Smith, for all of her help and insight. Her years of experience shine through as she helped guide me through this process.

Thank you to Anthony McClure and Taunee Besson for being my "cheer leaders" and offering their input every step of the way.

Thank you to Johnita Salerno for her friendship, feedback and awesome designs.

Catherine Cates
Frisco, TX
2014

Know How to Do It — Getting the Most Out of Your Outings

"Outings are so much more fun when we can savor them through our children's eyes." – Lawana Blackwell

Family outings are important for children in to two basic ways: children learn by doing and they love being with you.

Adventures allow children to touch, see, and feel their world. Exposing children to new adventures enhances their understanding of themselves and the world they live in. Self-esteem is born through mastering physical activities and continued through constant practice of learning processes.

For adults, an outing is one way to get to know the area in which you live. Through the preparation and execution of an outing, adults can advance their personal skills of organization, planning, and creative thinking. Outings allow adults to be in control of the day and give valuable opportunities to see their child in an exploratory and discovery mode.

Do not wait until your child is ready to relate the total experience before attempting an outing! Begin when your child is a newborn. Choose a location you are interested in and start a life-long bonding tradition.

Planning an Outing

FIRST STEP Think about where you want to go, remembering the physical ability and intellectual development of the child. Outings do not have to be long, complicated or to exotic places. With very young children, try discovering adventures within a mile radius of your home such as the local pet store or attend a story time at the library. Visits to nearby frame shops, grocery stores and nature walks are enjoyable. Special exhibits at the mall may also constitute an outing as do art classes and a trip to the hardware store.

SECOND STEP Mark it on the calendar immediately. This act almost guarantees the outing will proceed and confirms to you it is an important activity.

THIRD STEP Call or logon to the location's website to confirm hours open, fee (if any), and special concerns (available food services available, is the location stroller-friendly, etc.). Here are a few tips:

- **Call ahead to identify popular dates.** Be aware, many places schedule busloads of school children during the weekday or have increased attendance on reduced days. Ensure there aren't any special events or circumstances that may impede your visit (ie. construction/renovation/other events in the area). Also check the AroundTownKids.com coupon page for potential coupons: *www.AroundTownKidsFrisco.com/coupons.htm*

- **Don't expect to visit every animal, smell every flower on the trail, or see every artifact on a single visit.** Save some attractions for next time.

- **Consider joining or purchasing a membership at the location.** Memberships can save you money, help preserve the facility, and allow you to receive mailings of upcoming events.

Outing Length

A frequently asked question: "How much time should be spent on an outing?" Outing length is broken up into two distinct time elements; travel time and intellectual stimulation time. Using travel times as a single factor, plan your outing be no longer than 2-3 hours for almost every age. This allows for a maximum of an hour and a half from your front door to the location. Any travel time longer than this requires a seasoned adventurer and that includes you!

Intellectual stimulation time refers to the amount of time you spend with your children in conversations, hands-on involvements, and interactions at the location. Intellectual stimulation can be in the form of direct questions, relating comments, pushing buttons as part of a process, a little time to sketch or scrawl on paper, etc. The pocket(s) of time also includes "Kid Time," defined as the time a child spends intently observing a single object or activity of his choice. Following the path of an ant or practicing jumping over stones is important focusing time that should not be interrupted.

The time allotment for intellectual stimulation can be adjusted for each child's age, with these recommended guidelines:	
One year-olds	10 minutes
Two year-olds	10-15 minutes
Three year-olds	10-30 minutes
Four year-olds	30-40 minutes
Five year-olds	30-45 minutes
Six to Ten year-olds	40+ minutes
Eleven year-olds and beyond	50+ minutes

The intellectual stimulation time can be calculated over several nonconsecutive periods of time or may be achieved repeatedly during an outing. For example, a two year-old may be actively engaged for two minutes over five separate nonconsecutive periods, thereby intellectually stimulated for 10 minutes as suggested in the guideline chart above. Likewise, a five year-old may be focused on activities for half an hour at three different times during the outing. This measurement exceeds the guidelines for a five year-old. Note: these are only guidelines and your child may be able to sustain intellectual stimulation far longer than suggested or quite a bit less.

Is the Outing Over?

There are some sure clues when your outing is over. When your child is continually crying or becomes easily frustrated, this is a sign it is time to go home. If your child is asleep, his outing is over. (This might be a good time for you to visit a special display, or re-visit an artifact you are interested in while he sleeps in the stroller.) Older children may verbally tell you they "are done." And as important, when to feel mentally and/or physically tired, this is a sign the adventure is over. Save the rest of the location for another day.

Outing Evaluation

Record your thoughts of the outing and your interest in repeating the activity. Make note of any item(s) that may have made your outing a negative experience or those that enhanced your day. Children will not experience or learn everything the location has to offer on a single visit. Repeat visits are extremely valuable. With adults, children will see something different each time they visit. Consider scheduling to repeat a location at a four month interval. You'll be amazed at how much more they learn the next time! With your child, create a simple photo record from the day. Reviewing these photos can help remember your child's favorite location and stimulate conversation of past experiences.

Animals & Marine Life

Many children love animals and enjoy watching marine life swim around. Visiting animals and marine life exhibits can help teach children how to care for wildlife and grow a healthy respect for their lives and place on our Earth. On occasion, a child may have developed a fear of animals and be hesitant to visit up close. Going to the zoo, aquarium, or smaller animal and marine life exhibits will help a child overcome his anxieties.

Combine children's natural fascinations with animals with their early reading and writing skills by reading stories or picture books about animals.

Know Where to Go
Suggested Animal & Marine Life Locations in DFW

Bass Pro Outdoor World – Grapevine and Garland
www.basspro.com

Cabela's – Allen and Fort Worth
www.cabelas.com

Dallas Children's Aquarium at Fair Park - Dallas
www.childrensaquariumfairpark.com

Dallas World Aquarium, West End - Dallas
www.dwazoo.com

Dallas Zoo - Dallas
www.dallaszoo.com

Fort Worth Herd Cattle Drive – Stockyards, Fort Worth
www.stockyardsstation.com

Fort Worth Zoo - Fort Worth
www.fortworthzoo.org

Fossil Rim Wildlife Center – Glen Rose
www.fossilrim.com

Frank Buck Zoo - Gainesville
www.frankbuckzoo.com

In Sync Exotics Wildlife Rescue and Education Center - Wylie
www.insyncexotics.org

Mesquite Championship Rodeo - Mesquite
www.mesquiterodeo.com

Owens Spring Creek Farms – Richardson
www.bobevans.com

SeaLife Aquarium - Grapevine
www.visitsealife.com/Grapevine

Sharkarosa Wildlife Ranch - Pilot Point
www.sharkarosa.com

Stockyards Championship Rodeo - Fort Worth
www.stockyardsrodeo.com

Texas Freshwater Fishery Center - Athens
www.tpwd.state.tx.us/spdest/visitorcenters/tffc

What Your Kids Can Learn Here
Age Appropriate Activities for Animals & Marine Life

ONE YEAR OLDS

- Walk, run, climb stairs, cross bridges, and manipulate pathways to each exhibit.
- Listen to the animal/marine life sounds.
- Introduce new vocabulary including animal/marine life names, associated artifacts, and related concepts.
- Touch the living creatures.

TWOS & THREES

- Identify different colors found on animals/marine life.
- Ask: What do these animals/marine life eat?
- Touch and feel the animals/marine life body. Talk about fur, feathers, hide, hair, and scales.
- If possible, take a ride on an animal or swim with marine life.
- Count body parts that appear in sets: feet, legs, ears, eyes, etc.
- Emulate the sounds these creatures make.
- Draw your favorite animal/marine life.

FOURS & FIVES

- Learn about simple care of animals/marine life.
- Talk about camouflage and how it protects.
- Ask: What parts of animal/marine life allow it to move?
- Ask: Where do animals/marine life sleep?
- Ask: How do these animals/marine life help humans?
- Discover special animals/marine life that has played an important role in human lives.
- Consider getting your own animal/marine life as a pet or adopt a favorite creature from a zoo.
- Listen to a short talk from an animal/marine life caregiver or trainer.
- Learn the difference between wild and tame.
- Compare animals' feet and marine fins. Ask: What makes these perfect for each creature?

- Introduce seven habitats: prairie, grasslands, marine, rainforest, desert, arctic, and mountain.

- Discover specific characteristics of animal/marine life habitats.

- Ask: Where do these animals/marine life live in our world?

- Watch animal/marine life behaviors in their habitats. Record your observations.

- Identify enemies and its allies.

- Ask: How do these animals/marine life adapt to their environment?

- Learn about special medical care that is sometimes needed.

- Introduce new vocabulary: *species, extinct, habitat.*

- Create your own 3-D animal/marine life characterization using a variety of art supplies.

- Compare footprints and identify specific animal prints.

Animals & Marine Life Featured Destinations

Bass Pro Outdoor World

Dallas Children's Aquarium at Fair Park

Dallas Zoo

Fort Worth Zoo

Fossil Rim Wildlife Center

Bass Pro Outdoor World

972-724-2018 Grapevine or 469-221-2600 Garland, TX
2501 Bass Pro Drive, Grapevine, TX or 5001 Bass Pro Drive, Garland
www.basspro.com

WHAT: Retail sporting goods store hosting mounted animals

HOURS: Mon – Sat @ 9am - 10pm; Sun @ 10am – 9pm

ADMISSION: Free

Normally I would not advocate taking our youngest children to a retail shop as an outing, but I make an exception for Bass Pro Shops. This outdoor sporting goods store offers children a chance to see stuffed animals from the wild, live fish swimming in tanks and a pond, a waterfall and a variety of footprints pressed into the walkways throughout the store. You may even get to see a demonstration of fishing lures at the waterfall.

There are numerous outdoor sports represented here including fishing, hunting, camping, golf and archery. As you enter Bass Pro Outdoor World, pick up a store map and directory to help you find the areas you wish to show the children. Bring your camera or use your cell phone camera as there are special photo opportunities at various spots around the store.

NOTE: The following activities are based on the Grapevine store location.

TIPS FROM THE AROUND TOWN MOM

- ✓ *Amenities include: Snack area and restrooms.*

- ✓ *There is an electronic shooting gallery designed for older children and adults located by the Gift Shop.*

- ✓ *During the holidays the Easter Bunny and Santa are available for free photo opps. (Photos are also available for purchase). Bass Pro also offers free holiday crafts and activities during this time.*

- The boat and the animal carvings out front will catch the eye of a one year-old.
- Point out the stuffed animals perched along the walls.
- Watch the fish swimming at the foot of the waterfall.
- Introduce animal names: *buffalo, eagle, goat*

TWOS & THREES

- Make the sounds of the animals you see.
- Look at the floor as you walk around the store. Ask: Can you identify the animal's footprints you see?
- Look high and low. Ask: Can you find the mountain climbers? The huge shark? How many fish can you count?
- The waterfall will attract these children's attention. Take a walk around the base of the falls. Ask: What do you see?

FOURS & FIVES

- Climb aboard the boats and pretend to be the captain.
- At the waterfall, watch the fish swimming about. Using the chart posted, ask: Which fish can you identify?
- Go into the cave behind the waterfall. Look just below the water line and watch the water as it tumbles.
- Ask: Can you find the bronze sculpture "Riding the Big Fish"?
- Try your hand at mini golf at the putting green.

SIX & BEYOND

- Talk about outdoor sports like camping, fishing, archery and boating and associated safety.
- Try your hand at the archery range.
- Using the store map, find the areas located on the map.
- Point out all the different types of items in the store and ask: Where do all of these items come from? How did they get here?
- If you purchase something, explain the details of the receipt to your child.

Dallas Children's Aquarium

469-554-7340
1462 First Avenue, Dallas, TX
www.childrensaquariumfairpark.com/

WHAT: Historic Art Deco building at Fair Park featuring 375 species of marine and freshwater fish, reptiles, amphibians and invertebrates

HOURS: Daily 9am - 4:30pm

ADMISSION: $8/Adults; $6/Children (3-11 yrs) & seniors (65+); Ages 2 & under–Free

The Dallas Children's Aquarium was renovated and re-opened September 2010. One feature I noticed right away, and as a parent, I appreciated: it was designed with kids in mind. The interactive zones and exhibits are at eye-level so there's no standing on tippy-toes or boosting kids up to see. Well-lit placards include colorful signs to share interesting facts about each species on display. Exhibit halls are very spacious allowing plenty of room to maneuver strollers.

To captivate your children's attention there are many kid-friendly features including hands-on demonstrations, child-viewing windows, and touch tanks. Of special interest is an outdoor pavilion featuring Stingray Bay, a place to enjoy these majestic creatures as they glide about their tank.

Your kids will love the Dallas Children's Aquarium as it showcases the "greatest hits" of the sea, such as sea creatures from books and movies that are familiar to children. Perfect for preschoolers, this aquarium is small, but will not bore older children.

TIPS FROM THE AROUND TOWN MOM

✓ *Amenities include: Restrooms, water fountains, vending machine and gift shop with drinks for purchase.*

✓ *Food and drinks are allowed, but not in the touch tank areas or Stingray Bay.*

✓ *Weekly Fish Feeding Demonstration at 2:30pm – see website for schedule as each day features a different species.*

✓ *There is bench seating in the exhibit halls for a break.*

✓ *Look for a good photo opportunity at the giant fake octopus with long tentacles.*

- Watch aquatic animals swimming.
- Introduce different types of aquatic animals: sharks, sea turtles and jellyfish.
- Talk about the colors and shapes you see.
- Touch the resin-encased exhibit items (glass bottle, crab, oyster shell, pebbles, etc) below the octopus tentacles and point out the various textures – smooth, rough, bumpy etc.

TWOS & THREES

- Help your child find a "Nemo" or orange and white striped clown fish.
- Together, see if you find the upside-down jellyfish, the walking batfish, the lionfish, or the albino alligator.
- Point out the fish swimming in and out of the portholes in the lionfish tank.
- Visit the "touch tank" for live animal tactile exploration. Ask: Is the animal smooth or bumpy? Do the tentacles tickle you?
- If your child is agreeable, wrap your child in the giant fake octopus tentacles for a tactile experience.

FOURS & FIVES

- Discuss the natural habitat of aquatic animals.
- Find the moon jellies and the alligator snapping turtle.
- Ask: Are sea horses real? Can you find one in the aquarium?
- Point out the mushroom-shaped anemones.
- At Stingray Bay, look up and out the top windows for a unique perspective of the permanent Ferris wheel from the State Fair.

SIX & BEYOND

- Find signs on particular tanks indicating pregnant or endangered species.
- Ask: Are electric eels really electric?
- Discuss gills, fins, scales and tails and how they enable fish and other marine life to live in the sea.
- Ask: What are *predators*? Can you name some ocean predators?
- After visiting, consider allowing your child to have her own pet with reasonable expectation of its feeding and care.

Dallas Zoo

214-670-5656
650 So. R. L. Thornton Freeway, Dallas, TX
www.dallaszoo.com

WHAT: 1400+ mammals, birds, reptiles and amphibians.

HOURS: Open daily 9am – 5pm

ADMISSION: $15/Adults; $12/Seniors and children 3-11; Children age 2 and under are free. The Monorail is $3 per person ages 3 and up. $8/Parking

In recent years, The Dallas Zoo has spent a lot of time, resources and energy in updating many of its existing exhibits and animal habitats as well as adding some excellent exhibits such as the Savanna. And what a great outcome!

The Lacerte Children's Zoo is a very well done area featuring indoor learning centers focusing on specific animal topics. One of our favorites is the Nature Exchange. Bring in an artifact from nature or write a report on a personal interest from nature (animal or plant) and you are rewarded with nature points. These points can be saved or cashed in for unique artifacts such as shells, rocks, shark's tooth, wasp's nest, etc.

The Chimpanzee Forest allows up-close discovery of chimpanzees and their habitat. Be sure to stop by the Penguin Cove to see African Penguins as they swim. Other interests are the primates, larger animals and Reptile Discovery Center. There is a wonderful picnic spot in the middle of the zoo with tables and a giant turtle for the children to climb.

TIPS FROM THE AROUND TOWN MOM

- ✓ *Amenities include: Restrooms, water fountain, snack bar and gift shop.*
- ✓ *Rental strollers are available.*
- ✓ *Bring a few extra dollars to ride the carousel located at the zoo entry.*
- ✓ *Be sure to stop and get your photos taken in the wooden cut-outs.*
- ✓ *Bring Binoculars.*

- Go to the barn in the Lacerte Children's Zoo area to see lots of smaller animals, which children are encouraged to touch.
- There is plenty of room to practice gross motor skills in the playground area.
- At the playground, play peek-a-boo in the tree "tunnels."
- Using simple vocabulary, name specific animals, colors of their skin, and describe their outer coats.

- Visit the Lacerte Children's Zoo. Watch the koi fish swimming in the large tank. Ask: Are all the fish orange?
- Watch the meerkats popping up from the ground. Ask: Where might they pop up next?
- Count the number of giraffes.
- Enter the petting zoo in the Lacerte Children's Zoo to feed the goats, sheep, and other animals.
- Twos & Threes will enjoy the larger animals in the African Savanna exhibit, The Primate exhibit, the Chimpanzee Forest and those in the Reptile Discovery Center.

- The monorail is a great way to start the day and see a different perspective of the zoo and the animals.
- The Reptile Discovery Center has some hands-on learning activities designed for these children.
- Ask: Can you find the lemurs?
- Enter the bird sanctuary in the Lacerte Children's Zoo to watch the birds. Bring binoculars!
- Take some time for your child to draw their favorite animals.

- Ride the DART Light Rail System to the Zoo.
- Visit the Reptile Discovery Center and speak with the zoologist. Learn about his job and his qualifications.
- Take a camera and shoot photographs of interesting animals.
- Discuss the eating and sleeping habits of your favorite animal species.
- Discover regular routines of feeding, grooming, and entertainment of the animals. Ask: Do animals get sick? How are they cared for at this zoo?

Fort Worth Zoo

817-871-7050
1989 Colonial Parkway, Fort Worth, TX
www.fortworthzoo.com

WHAT: Over 5,000 animals on 58+ acres.

HOURS: Open daily 10am – 5pm

ADMISSION: $12/Adults; $9/Seniors & Children 3-12; Children 2 and under - Free. Half-price admission on Wednesday. $5/Parking

There are 3 areas of the zoo you don't want to miss – the World of Primates, the penguins and *Texas Wild!* The primate area is the best of its kind with thick Plexiglas windows to allow children to see the animals move about in their natural habitat both inside and outside. Other areas to add to your list include the *Herpetarium, Australian Outback,* children's petting zoo, *Insect Gallery,* and *Cheetah* exhibits.

Visit the African and rockhopper penguins at the indoor penguin exhibit. *Wild Encounters,* a daily stage show, offers a close-up look at animals with a show-and-tell commentary by zoo employees.

The Fort Worth Zoo also includes the Texas Nature Traders program whereby children can bring in nature artifacts (fossils, rocks, plants etc) to exchange for points which can be redeemed at the Nature Trader Inventory.

TIPS FROM THE AROUND TOWN MOM

✓ *Amenities include: Restrooms, water fountains, gift shop and snack bar*

✓ *Strollers, double strollers and even motorized scooters are available for rent at the front gate.*

✓ *Bring a few extra dollars for the attractions such as the Country Carousel located in Texas Wild, the Yellow Rose Express Train, The Wild West Shooting Gallery, the Hurricane and Tornado Simulators and Tasmanian Tower.*

✓ *Use the binoculars provided wherever you can (or bring your own) to see the animals up close.*

- The *World of Primates* hosting an indoor tropical rain forest may catch the eye of the one year-old.
- Children will enjoy watching animals of any kind - especially if the animals are in motion. Try the *Aquarium* and *African Savannah* and *Texas Wild!*, specifically.
- Emulate the sounds of the animals.
- Identify each animal by name.

TWOS & THREES

- The *Petting Corral* in *Texas Wild!* is a must-see for kids this age and will allow children to pet goats, sheep, pigs, etc, in a confined area.
- Ask: Can you find the Meerkats, the termite mounds and the pink flamingoes?
- Compare animals you see, differences and similarities.
- In *Texas Wild!* touch the fish and sea creatures at the Texas Coast region. Ask: Does it smell like the seashore?
- Ask: Can you find the kangaroos?

FOURS & FIVES

- While at the *Asian Falls* and African *Savannah*, talk about animal's feet. Ask: Are they hoofed? Webbed? Flat?
- Ask: If you had this animal for a pet, where would it sleep?
- Discuss camouflage and how animals and reptiles hide from their prey. Ask: Who is their prey?
- Play "I Spy" to find the rhinos, the giraffes, the penguins and the white tiger.
- Take turns making faces at the monkeys and chimps to see who can get them to look back at you first.

SIX & BEYOND

- Introduce new vocabulary: *scavenger, prey, conservation*.
- Discuss extinction.
- Describe the savannah habitat and identify the attributes animals must have to live there.
- Explain the differences between a reptile and amphibian.
- Watch the big cats. Ask: Are they sleeping? Take the opportunity to discuss nocturnal species and specific adaptations they require.

Fossil Rim Wildlife Center

254-897-2960
2155 CR 2008, Glen Rose, TX
www.fossilrim.com

WHAT: 9-mile drive-through Safari Park and petting zoo. Fossil Rim has over 1000 animals representing 50 species living peacefully on 1700 acres.

HOURS: Vary by the season – see website.

ADMISSION: Prices vary per day and season – see website.

Going to Fossil Rim is a wonderful chance for children to experience animals in their natural habitat and see them "up close and personal" as you drive the 9-mile route through their living spaces. Fossil Rim has done an excellent job in their conservation efforts. This truly is a gem.

Use the map and animal photo ID guide as a tool to educate your children on the types of animals present on the tour. Kids will love to identify animals. If you have a child who likes to "check things off" like mine does, they will enjoy checking off the animals they have seen along the route.

To further enhance your experience, consider packing a picnic lunch. There are picnic tables at the halfway point and plenty of shade. Bring binoculars.

TIPS FROM THE AROUND TOWN MOM

✓ *Amenities include: Restrooms and gift shop.*

✓ ***USE THE RESTROOMS*** *in the visitor center before you begin your journey. There are no more restrooms until you reach the half way point, which can take a while, depending on traffic and your pace.*

✓ *Also at the halfway point is a petting zoo (Children's Animal Center) and gift shop. Let the kids out to see the animals up close and stretch your legs. There is plenty of open space to burn off some energy!*

✓ *Buying the animal feed ($8/bag) is worth every penny as you see your children squeal with delight while feeding the animals.*

✓ *Consider taking a special tour, the early morning, at dusk, or a behind-the-scenes tour so see a different view of these creatures.*

- The Children's Animal Center will be the highlight for these children—allow them to motor around.
- Sights and smells of these animals will stimulate the brain cells.
- Identify each animal by name.
- Allow touching and describe how each animal feels with simple vocabulary: *soft, rough, smooth,* etc.

- During the 9.5 mile drive, play "I Spy" using a variety of objects: specific animals, buildings, colors, and foliage.
- Use the animal photographs in the brochure to check off each creature as it is observed in their habitats.
- At the Children's Animal Center, talk about these animals in terms of sizes and heights to other animals and themselves. Use vocabulary - bigger, smaller, same size.
- Identify colors, and count legs, wings, beaks, hooves, etc.
- If available, try feeding one of the animals.

- The 9.5 mile car ride through the trails will interest this age, allowing them to observe animals in their natural habitat, and not so close and personal.
- Try feeding an animal out the vehicle window. Talk about how this experience feels.
- Use binoculars to see animals that may be off in the distance.
- Create a simple chart with boxes labeled "feathers," "hooves," "horns," "hide," "beaks," etc. and have your child count the number of animals they see with these characteristics.
- At the Children's Animal Center, talk about their enclosures and how this protects them from dangers.

- Pay attention to the types of habitats and environments these animals need to survive. Ask: What is special about them?
- Ask: How do plants play a role in the lifestyles of certain animals?
- Using a camera, allow your child to take photographs of their favorites for a later study. This can include a bit of journaling or a blog for other children to follow.
- Ask: What is a zoologist? Why are they important at a place like this?
- Talk about the parts of the world where these animals would be found and identify these locations on a world map.

Art not only gets kids thinking creatively, it allows them to see things from different perspectives, building important life skills.

Visual, Performing & Theatrical Art:

SECTION I
Art Galleries, Art Museums & Sculptures

Young children are exposed to art for the first time at home with coloring books and paints. Because art can be found almost anywhere, you can expand their portfolios of exploration during nature walks, urban settings, student works at colleges and universities, and many brick and mortar locations. The most traditional places for art appreciation are art museums themselves but because most discourage touching, visit shops where art and framing services are for purchase. These locations serve as good starting places to introduce art to your youngest because they do not have penalties for tactile exploration.

Children who experience art are exposed to a myriad of styles, artists, mediums and the emotional connections that invoke feelings and thought. Viewing art helps young children with limited vocabulary express their feelings and thoughts.

When visiting, encourage your child to bring a clipboard, paper, and several colored pencils. Ask your child to draw while viewing works. Emulating on paper what he sees practices an important focusing skill and requires him to create a relationship between himself and the works of art in front of him.

Know Where to Go
Suggested Art Galleries, Art Museums & Sculptures in DFW

African American Museum – Fair Park, Dallas
www.aamdallas.org

Altermann & Morris Gallery – Dallas
www.altermann.com

Amon Carter Museum – Fort Worth
www.cartermuseum.com

Arlington Museum of Art – Arlington
www.arlingtonmuseum.org

Central Park – Frisco
*www.friscofun.org/parks/parks/
Pages/CentralPark.aspx*

Crow Collection of Asian Art – Dallas
www.crowcollection.org

Dallas Center of Contemporary Arts – Dallas
www.dallascontemporary.org

Dallas Museum of Art – Dallas
www.dallasmuseumofart.org

Frolicking Pixies Sculpture – Lakeside Historical District, Dallas
www.waymarking.com

Ivanffy-Uhler Gallery – Dallas
www.ivanffyuhler.com

Kimbell Art Museum – Fort Worth
www.kimbellart.org

Kittrell/Riffkind Art Glass – Addison
www.kittrellriffkind.com

Latino Cultural Center – Dallas
*www.dallasculture.org/latinocultur
alcenter*

Meadows Museum – Highland Park
www.meadowsmuseumdallas.org

Modern Art Museum of Fort Worth – Fort Worth
www.themodern.org

Museum of Biblical Arts – Dallas
www.biblicalarts.org

Museum of Geometric & MADI Art – Dallas
www.geometricmadimuseum.org

Nasher Sculpture Center – Dallas
www.nashersculpturecenter.org

Pioneer Plaza – Dallas
www.dallasconventioncenter.com

Sid Richardson Collection of Western Art – Fort Worth
www.sidrichardsonmuseum.org

South Dallas Cultural Center – Dallas
*www.dallasculture.org/sdcultural
center*

Texas Sculpture Garden – Frisco
www.texassculpturegarden.com

The Mustangs of Las Colinas – Irving
www.mustangsoflascolinas.com

UT Southwestern Medical Center – Dallas
www.utsouthwestern.edu

Valley House Gallery & Sculpture Gardens – Dallas
www.valleyhouse.com

White Rock Lake Museum – Dallas
www.whiterocklakemuseum.org

Wyndham Anatole Hotel Art Study – Dallas
*www3.hilton.com/en/hotels/texas/
hilton-anatole-DFWANHH/index.html*

What Your Kids Can Learn Here
Age Appropriate Activities for Art Galleries, Art Museums & Sculptures

ONE YEAR OLDS

- Walk through the hallways and gallery rooms, practicing walking indoors and using quiet voices.
- Identify colors and simple shapes.
- Talk about the objects your child sees in the art work.
- If available, visit the outdoor sculptures and gently touch the art works.

TWOS & THREES

- Teach basic etiquette skills for indoor, quiet locations.
- Talk about the colors and shapes as they relate to general themes throughout the art work.
- Play "I Spy" with objects within the art.
- Talk about what the main subject is doing.
- Draw a favorite painting or sculpture.
- Recreate a 3D art work.

FOURS & FIVES

- Ask: Is the art work real or imagined?
- Identify styles and techniques within certain works.
- Distinguish between different art mediums: metal works, wood carving, clay, oil paints, textiles, etc.
- Try to imagine what the main subject was doing before appearing in the art work.
- Ask: Where might the subject go if he left this art work?
- Ask: What do you think about the art you see?

SIX & BEYOND

- Continue to visit as many art exhibits as possible and compare locations.
- Identify different tools used to create the works.
- Define a favorite style and research the artist's life.
- Begin to develop your own artistic style.
- Create original art projects using a variety of mediums including paint, clay, newspaper, photography, pastels, recycled items, fabric, and beading.
- Take an art class offered by an art museum or studio.

Artistic creations begin with planning and problem solving such as, "How do I turn this clay into sculpture?"

Art Galleries, Art Museums & Sculptures Featured Destinations

Crow Collection of Asian Art

Dallas Museum of Art

Kimbell Art Museum

Nasher Sculpture Center

The Mustangs of Las Colinas

Crow Collection of Asian Art

214-979-6430
2010 Flora Street, Dallas TX
www.crowcollection.org

WHAT: Display of art from China, Japan, India, and Southeast Asia

HOURS: Tues–Thurs @ 10am–9pm; Fri & Sat @ 10am–6pm; Sun @ 12pm–6pm

ADMISSION: Free; donations accepted

Who would've thought there would be an art collection inside an office building complex? This exhibit will take your breath away! The art works date from 3,500 BC to the early 20th century. Some pieces will rotate to allow the entire collection of 7,000 artifacts to be shown 550 pieces at a time. Each room offers artifacts from different Asian and Indian cultures and the music piped overhead further defines each geographic region. I like this museum because many of the artifacts are not enclosed in glass. This allows for closer examination and study.

There are so many exquisite pieces to see you will want to introduce children to every piece. Notice the varied techniques used to create the works (brushing, painting, carving, molding, etc.), and discuss them with children. Don't miss the 2,000 pound bronze Confucius seated outside the entrance. This museum definitely deserves repeat visits!

The outside sculpture garden features some new pieces including the Shi of East and West, Deified Laozi, and Jain Temple Columns. Do not miss this additional area when visiting the Crow Collection of Asian Art.

This outing makes a great compliment to a cultural diverse neighborhood market study.

TIPS FROM THE AROUND TOWN MOM

- ✓ *Amenities include: Restrooms available.*
- ✓ *Stroller friendly – there are elevators*
- ✓ *Exhibits do change so check The Around Town Kids event calendar: www.AroundTownKidsFrisco.com/events.htm*
- ✓ *iPads are provided to explore virtual cultures and landscapes.*
- ✓ *Touching of the artwork is not allowed although some pieces do not have signs.*

Inside:

- Maneuver around the displays, walk up the stairs to improve gross motor skills.
- Introduce "big" and "little" as it relates to artifacts such as the little jade carvings and the big Indian façade.
- Get an up close look at Buddha, the Indian horse, and large vases.

Outside: Practice walking, jumping, and moving around sculptures.

Inside:

- Identify different animals seen throughout this museum.
- Within the Chinese arts, introduce which sculpture is the Buddha.
- Point out the facial expressions in the art pieces. Talk about how some of the pieces show their emotions.
- Ask: Can you find the Hindu elephant - the ganesha?
- Count the arms on Indian characters. Ask: What could you do with so many arms?

Outside: Ring the large Edo period bell and listen to its deep tone.

Inside:

- Listen to the background music. Ask: How is it different for each culture?
- Study maps of geographic regions and familiarize yourself with the shapes of the countries.
- Ask: Can you find the pagoda with the seven stories of bells? The ivory toad?
- Ask: Can you "read" the stories from the large Japanese screens?
- Ask: What materials are used in the art works?

Outside: Find the Makara sculpture and talk about its body parts. Identify which animals are represented within.

Inside:

- Identify the shapes of India, China and Japan. Identify the water surrounding these locations.
- Ask: How is Indian culture different or the same from your own?
- Let kids sit on the meditation mat and be still. Try it at home and perhaps strike a yoga pose.
- At home use red clay and re-create the red jade pieces at the museum.

Outside: Visit the Sweepers sculpture and talk about this daily important chore performed by monks. Ask: What chores do you perform daily and why are they important?

Dallas Museum of Art

214-922-1200
1717 N. Harwood Street, Dallas, TX
www.dallasmuseumofart.org

WHAT: Art and artifacts from nearly all cultures

HOURS: Tues–Wed @ 11am–5pm; Thurs @ 11am–9pm; Fri, Sat & Sun @ 11am–5pm; Closed Mondays

ADMISSION: Free General Admission; Special Exhibit Pricing: $16/Adults; $14/Seniors; $12/Students; 11 and under - Free

The Dallas Museum of Art is now FREE! Only special exhibits require a fee. The museum caters to children with its Young Learners Gallery designed for ages five – eight years old and Arturo's Nest, specific to one to four year olds. The main museum will hold the attention of children because of its variety of exhibits.

The re-designed Young Learners Gallery is "nirvana" for those looking to engage and educate their children about art starting at the earliest of ages. They must have had you, the educated parent, in mind when they designed it. To guide your children through the area, there are "talking points" and placards offering suggestions to parents. The Young Learners Gallery features a children's library, art games, family films and computer activities related to art.

Try a picnic in the sculpture garden, experience the water walls, and point out the sculpture trees. Participate in the weekend art offered by the museum where children are invited to create art to mirror the current exhibit. This is a creative way to introduce art and allow children to develop their talents in different mediums.

TIPS FROM THE AROUND TOWN MOM

✓ *Amenities include: Water fountains, restrooms and a restaurant, the DMA Café.*

✓ *Baby comfort station is available for nursing mothers in the Center for Creative Connections.*

✓ *Strollers, diaper bags and frontal baby carriers are welcome.*

✓ *Backpacks are not permitted.*

✓ *smART phone tours are available to access new and interactive content.*

✓ *Sign up to be a "member," then you can text the exhibit codes you see during your visit. Points accumulate to win things such as a free café lunch etc.*

✓ *Arturo's Nest has Spanish translations.*

- The *Young Learners Gallery* Discovery Room offers tactile experiences such as the grass wall and the chain curtain.
- Peek into the mirrors and make faces.
- Scrawl on the white board.
- Visit *Arturo's Nest* for tactile exploration with stuffed animals, puppets, and blocks, kinesthetic opportunities for crawling and climbing, and hands-on simple art creations.

TWOS & THREES

- In *Arturo's Nest* "write" a letter to Arturo, the colorful parrot, and put it in the mailbox.
- In *Arturo's Nest* put on a puppet show.
- Introduce exhibits from the main gallery to these children and talk about shapes, colors and objects they see.
- Measure outdoor sculpture with hands and bodies.
- While the *Young Learners Gallery* is designed for ages 5 – 8 yrs, there are many tactile activities for this age including the Lego™ wall.

FOURS & FIVES

- *Young Learners Gallery*, designed for ages 5-8, encourages original art works on the white board and participation in the activities.
- Within the main museum, there are several exhibits (sculpture, painting and cultural artifacts) for more mature five year-olds.
- Discuss what the subjects might be thinking or where they are going.
- Identify cultural identities, for example, woodcarvings of Asian art and stone carvings of the Mayans.
- Talk about art work and emotions. Ask: How does the art make you feel? What does it remind you of?

SIX & BEYOND

- Systematically visit each gallery in this museum and learn about geographical and cultural artifacts.
- Combine this trip with an outing to one of the cultural food markets. (For example: study Japanese art in the museum, then go to a Japanese food market for a continued study)
- Stop in the "Art Spot," stocked with pencils and scissors, to draw your own art or imitate art in the museum.
- Participate in their "Art Exchange" program and "make one, take one."
- At home, emulate a favorite style and hang your project on the wall with an artist placard.

Kimbell Art Museum

817-332-8451
3333 Camp Bowie Blvd., Fort Worth, TX
www.kimbellart.org

WHAT: 350 pieces of ancient to modern art in the permanent collection

HOURS: Tues–Thurs @ 10am–5pm; Fri @ 12pm–8pm; Sat @ 10am–5pm; Sunday @ 12pm–5pm; Closed Mondays.

ADMISSION: General Admission is Free. Special Exhibit Pricing: $18/Adults; $16/Seniors; $14/Children 6 – 11 yrs; Under 6 - Free. Special Exhibit fees subject to change. Please see museum website for current prices.

The Kimbell Art Museum exhibits art from a variety of periods. While the permanent collection includes 350 pieces of art, this museum hosts many outstanding special exhibits from all over the world.

The Kimbell has a fun way to introduce children to the code of conduct at art museums. Stop by the downstairs Information Desk, mention "Kimbell Kids," and list one important museum rule to receive a free "Kimbell Kids" sticker. As a parent this nifty program can make your job a little easier to enforce rules such as no touching the artworks, no running, use "inside voices" etc.

To encourage children's interest, the Kimbell has picture cards, or family gallery guides which can be borrowed from the Information Desk, highlighting Kimbell masterpieces in the permanent collection. Parents can use the discussion questions on these flip cards as conversation starters and kids will enjoy reading the fun facts. Use these laminated images for pointing out details without getting too close to the original artworks. A gallery guide is available for special exhibits to introduce children to particular art pieces.

TIPS FROM THE AROUND TOWN MOM

✓ *Amenities include: Restrooms, water fountains and Buffet Restaurant*

✓ *Strollers are allowed but children may not push them.*

✓ *Backpacks and other large items must be stored at the Parcel check.*

✓ *Pencils and sketchbooks are allowed, but parents must carry them. Pens and other coloring materials are prohibited in the galleries.*

✓ *Bring a picnic and rest in the beautiful landscaped back garden.*

- Small waterways make a tempting place to run their fingers and the textured walkways give those little legs a challenge.
- The outside marble stairs will keep the one-year-old busy.
- Hold close and identify what you see using simple words.

- Bright colors and shapes catch their eyes in the gallery adjacent to the restaurant.
- Go to the center courtyard and visit the sculpture.
- Discover the sculpture and exhibits downstairs, at the main entrance, and discuss their shape and realism.
- Count the number of pictures containing people.

- These children will detect artists' stylistic differences and are willing to talk about what they see.
- The ancient sculpture statues in the entry hall make interesting conversation about who the people were and their body ornamentation.
- Look for special exhibits offered by the museum to visit.
- Ask: Can you find "Running Flower" sculpture?
- Clipboards, paper and colored pencils are tools not to be forgotten. The variety of art displayed allows a child to find something to emulate. Save time for your child to draw their favorite artwork.

- Use the picture cards as a "seek and find" activity to locate and help identify types of artwork in the permanent collection such as sculptures, portraits etc.
- Discuss different artistic techniques.
- Introduce new vocabulary: *stippling, impressionism, cubism, water colors*.
- Ask: Which was your favorite artwork and why?
- At home start an artwork collection with posters or postcards purchased at the gift shop.

Nasher Sculpture Center

214-242-5153
2001 Flora St, Dallas TX
www.nashersculpturecenter.org

WHAT: Over 300 sculptures and paintings

HOURS: 11am–5pm every day except CLOSED on MONDAYS

ADMISSION: $10/Adults; $7/Seniors; Kids 12 & under are Free

Situated in the heart of the Dallas Arts District, the Nasher Sculpture Center offers unique views of the Dallas cityscape. Turn one direction and you can see the Dallas Museum of Art. Turn another direction and view the Dallas Symphony Center. Across the street is the Crow Museum of Asian Art. Art opportunities abound, but don't try to do them all in one day with small children.

You may not consider the Nasher Sculpture Center as an outing for children, but it is. The first Saturdays of the month cater specifically to children when admission is free to everyone. Themed activities include family tours, hands-on craft, take home art activities, scavenger hunt and story time led by the Dallas Public Library affiliates. For more information on their events see their website or the AroundTownKids.com event calendar: *www.AroundTownKidsFrisco.com/events.htm*

The back garden is absolutely lovely, an oasis in an urban environment. With plenty of shade trees, fountains and wide open spaces, it is the perfect setting for the sculptures. Young children will love being outdoors and having "room to roam." If you have to pick and choose between the indoor spaces and outdoors, if the weather is good, pick the outdoors to keep your child entertained.

TIPS FROM THE AROUND TOWN MOM

- ✓ *Amenities include: Restrooms, water fountains, gift shop and Café featuring the cuisine of Wolfgang Puck.*

- ✓ *Touching is not allowed on the sculptures.*

- ✓ *Admission is half price on days when exhibits are changed.*

- ✓ *Go to NorthPark Mall to see additional sculptures and modern art. It will keep your child's memory fresh on sculpture and build "recall."*

- ✓ *No backpacks or large purses allowed. They can be checked in at the front desk.*

- Walk in the wide open spaces in the back outdoor garden.
- Practice walking up and down the stairs in the gallery.
- Watch the birds and other small wildlife in the garden.
- Listen to the fountains.

Outside:

- While viewing the sculpture, "Tower of Lace," ask: Is this sculpture taller than you? What colors do you see?
- View the sculpture of the group of people. Ask: What is the weather? What are they wearing? Can you identify some of the items? (ex. purse, high heels, buttons etc.)

Inside:

- Count the rectangles.
- Identify shapes.
- Play "I Spy."

Inside:

- Ask: Is this sculpture heavier than you?
- Ask: How did this sculpture get here?
- Introduce new vocabulary: *bronze, granite, mould, mask*

Outside:

- View the 2-row sculpture of people with no heads called "The Bronze Crowd." Ask: Is this real?
- Find the slate stone path. Ask: Why do you think the path ends?
- Choose a spot and strike your own pose, be your own sculpture.

Inside:

- At the sculpture "Quantum Cloud XX: Tornado," ask: What do you see in this sculpture?
- At the sculpture, "The Serf," ask: What is this sculpture made of?
- Using a clipboard or notebook, encourage our child to draw some of the sculptures as they are or as the child might want them to be.

Outside:

- Build a story around the sculpture of the group of people.
- Ask: What do you think the woman in the sculpture called, "Night" is thinking?
- When in the backyard garden, ask: Can you identify the other buildings in the Arts District?

The Mustangs of Las Colinas

972-869-9047
5205 N. O'Connor Drive, Irving, TX
www.mustangsoflascolinas.com

WHAT: Bronze sculpture of nine mustangs running in a stream

HOURS: Outside sculpture open daily. Museum open Wed–Sat @ 11am–5pm

ADMISSION: Free

Located in Williams Square, this outdoor location features the largest equestrian sculpture in the world, nine mustangs crossing a stream. Its sheer size and weight put viewers in awe. Three large pink granite buildings loom over the square where the mustangs ride. A quiet plaza surrounds the sculpture. This is a great tourist destination if you have guests in from out of town.

Don't miss the 20-minute video about the making of these lovely mustangs by African wild life artist Robert Glen. The video is shown in the small photographic museum that is located in the base of the West Tower.

TIPS FROM THE AROUND TOWN MOM

- ✓ *Amenities include: Restrooms and gift shop in museum building*

- ✓ *Bring a picnic and enjoy the scenery*

- ✓ *After the sculpture, visit the canals, take a gondola ride, or perhaps a run up Brune Hill to the Marble Cow Sculpture.*

- Children this age will want to run and explore in this large open area.
- Wet clothes are almost certain for this age.
- Count the mustangs and touch them.

- Talk with the child to identify the mustangs.
- Ask: Where do you think they are running?
- Ask: How do the mustangs feel?
- Ask: What expressions do they portray?
- In the museum, find and touch the huge mustang on the wall.

- Discuss the aspect of bronze and why the artist may have chosen this type of material to do the sculpture.
- Compare this with other bronze or sculpture the child has seen.
- Ask: Which horse do you think is the leader? Which are the colts?
- In the museum, search for other sculptures created by this famous artist.

- Ask: Why was this particular sculpture chosen for this location? What is its meaning?
- Try a paper rubbing of the horses.
- Ask: How many steps does it take to create a bronze sculpture cast?
- Ask: Who was the artist of these magnificent pieces? Where did he live? Did his homeland play a role in his creative talents? How?
- Learn about preservation of these outdoor sculptures.

Children learn to break down the mechanics of body language by watching or participating in live theater and even puppet shows.

Visual, Performing & Theatrical Art:

SECTION II
Live Theatrical Performances & Puppet Shows

You may be wondering about the appropriateness of live theatre performances and formal puppet shows for young children. My recommendation is that a child be at least three years old before attempting these mediums and those younger children can attend puppet shows at library story times and other informal settings where exiting before the end is expected. For a first time live theatre performance for a three year-old, the story should be one she already knows and the performance short in length. The more performances she attends the better she is able to extend her focus until she is finally able to stay for the entire performance. A seasoned three year-old may still need to exit early and this should be expected.

To get the maximum benefit and enjoyment with children at a live theatre performance or puppet show, the following tips are helpful:

- Be sure your child is rested and fed before the show.
- Many shows are performed without house lighting so the theatre may be darkened - prepare your child for this.
- If the performance is advertised with an "adapted by…" note, call ahead and see what changes have been made to the original script.
- Sometimes props like gongs, tiny firecrackers and loud musical horns are part of the show.
- Try to avoid evening performances with young children.
- Often performers will greet their audience and sign programs. However, if your child is not interested in getting close to these strangers, do not insist.

Know Where to Go
Suggested Live Theatrical Performances & Puppet Shows in DFW

ArtCentre of Plano – Plano
www.artcentreofplano.org

Artisan Theatre - Hurst
www.artisanct.com

Dallas Children's Theatre - Dallas
www.dct.org

Dallas Puppet Theater – check website for performance locations
www.puppetry.org

Garland Performing Arts Center – Garland
www.garlandarts.com

Irving Arts Center – Irving
www.irvingartscenter.com

Kathy Burks Theatre and Puppetry Arts – check website for performance locations
www.kathyburkspuppets.com

Le Theatre de Marionette – check website for performance locations
www.letheatredemarionette.com

Mesquite Art Center – Mesquite
www.cityofmesquite.com/artsweb

Plano Children's Theatre - Plano
www.planochildrenstheatre.org

Richardson's Children's Theatre – Richardson
www.richardsonchildrenstheatre.net

Theatre Coppell - Coppell
www.theatrecoppell.com

The Wylie Theatre - Dallas
www.dallastheatercenter.com

What Your Kids Can Learn Here
Age Appropriate Activities for Live Theatrical Performances & Puppet Shows

ONE YEAR OLDS

Live theatre:
- I do not recommend a child this young attend a live performance unless it is part of a family outing.
- Hold her close and whisper characters' names and sing songs with her as long as she will stay in her seat.

Puppet arts:
- This art may scare a child because one year-olds do not distinguish between real and fantasy.
- This child may be entertained for a short period of time but be prepared to leave before the performance is finished.

TWOS & THREES

Live Theatre:
- Prepare your child to expect the lights to go out.
- Keep your child's attention by quietly whispering short commentaries about the characters and their costumes.
- As the show is in progress, whisper what will happen next.
- Afterwards, ask: Can you remember the different parts of the story?

Puppet Arts:
- Puppets with strings will fascinate older TWOS & THREES.
- Talk about the audiences' rules before a show.
- While in progress, whisper: Do you know what will happen next?
- Whisper about the characters in the story, how they are dressed and the scenery.

FOURS & FIVES

Live Theatre:
- Before the performance, read the story together and imagine what the characters will look like on the stage.
- Suggest dressing up for the event in storybook costumes matching the characters.
- Purchase a program book or souvenir to remember the event.
- Take photographs, if permissible.
- Afterwards, talk about the performance, stage scenery and music.

Puppet Arts:

- This activity is perfect for children with active imaginations.
- Watch the backdrops move in and out of place.
- Afterwards, go back stage for a behind-the-scenes look at puppetry magic and ask questions of the puppeteers.
- Five-year-olds may be interested in how these puppets work and how certain maneuvers are performed.
- Ask: Do you know a different ending of the story?
- Ask: Can you re-tell the whole story?

SIX & BEYOND

Live Theatre:

- If the child wishes, bring a special autograph book to collect signatures from the performers. This will be especially nice as you meet popular celebrities.
- Sign up for theatre performance training offered by many theatre groups.

Puppet Arts:

- Try making puppets at home and put on your own puppet show.
- Many theatres offer classes on puppeteers.
- Participate in a production of a local puppet show.
- Choose a famous puppet show and perform it at school or scout event.
- Continue to see a variety of shows and create a blog about the experiences for others to add to their adventures list.

Visual, Performing & Theatrical Art:

SECTION III
Story Time

Story time is one of the most important activities you can do with your child – of any age. No one is too young to listen to a story; the amount of time you read aloud simply depends on the child's age and attention span. Unfortunately many parents stop reading aloud to their child once he masters the early primers for himself. It is at this precise time that parents should continue to read aloud. Reading aloud is a valuable tool for your child's continued interest in reading and comprehension success.

When reading at home, find a comfortable place and snuggle. Turn off the cell phone and don't answer the door. This shows your child that reading with him is a valuable and important time not to be disturbed. Regardless of the age of your listener, when reading aloud, stop at vocabulary words that may be complicated and ask their meaning. Talk about how a particular word is a good one for the sentence. Ask your listener what will happen next in the story.

When attending a library or bookstore reading, anticipate the types of stories to be read and talk to your child about what they will hear. ("This is the month of October. I think the librarian will read stories about leaves or pumpkins. What do you think?"). After the story time, check out a few of the same books that were read to review the stories at home.

There are different levels of listeners; pre-readers, beginning readers, intermediate readers and advanced readers and the following section describes these levels and gives some suggestions of the types of books these listeners may enjoy.

Pre-readers are those who enjoy listening to stories but are not yet reading words. Choose picture books, starting with cloth books for the youngest. Introduce board books, Touch-n-Feel books, Seek-n-Find books, and Lift-n-Flap books for children one to three. Teach your child how to care for books beginning with not stepping on or throwing them. Although the child is not reading the text, make a point to tell him the name of the author and the illustrator.

Beginning readers, children ages four through six years-old, can be ready to start identifying letters, learning the sound of letters, and reading simple words. Introduce puzzle books, Pop-Up and Pull-Tab books, Create-Your-Own-Ending books. A fundamental beginning reader skill is the picture walk. During a picture walk, look at the illustrations without reading the text. Turn each page slowly asking your child to tell you what he sees on each page. Just before you get to the end of the book, ask him how he thinks the picture story will end. See if he is right. When you have reached the end of the book, ask him to guess what the title might be. Introduce the table of contents and title page of each book.

Early readers are reading words, simple sentences and developing comprehension skills. Read aloud books with lots of pictures with one or two sentences on a page. Early readers will quickly request you read aloud short chapter books. After you have finished reading a story, ask him to re-tell the story in his own words. Use the pictures and simple words to correct him if needed. Discuss the table of contents in greater detail. Ask: On what page does chapter 2 begin? On what page does chapter 4 end?

With a greater developed comprehension, intermediate readers are enjoying independent reading of longer chapter books with fewer illustrations. Continue to read aloud stories with numerous characters, multiple settings and lots of action. Introduce the index, glossary, and copyright page. Ask the intermediate reader to select a title for you to read aloud and expect their attention to be 30 minutes or more. Encourage quiet reading time each day and continue to read aloud to them routinely.

Advanced readers are reading a variety of text including newspapers, magazines, maps, instructions, TV guides, movie selections, menus, poetry, etc. These children read for pleasure, school research, and information gathering. They are aware of special book honors like Caldecott and Newberry Medal awards. Read aloud some of your favorite multi-chaptered, non-illustrated classics. These books should not be completed in a single sitting but continued on over several nights or even weeks.

Just a word on reading text messages. Text messages often contain a language all unto itself. Using letters to mean full phrases (such as "LOL" - "laugh out loud") or single letter to mean a full word ("u" - "you" or "c" - "see") should not be confused with verbal conversation or take the place of spelling skills. Share this language with your child but do not allow it to be a substitute for good reading and writing skills. Or some1 may LOL at UR child's XPENS, GI?

What Your Kids Can Learn Here
Age Appropriate Activities for Story Time

ONE YEAR OLDS

- Begin visits to the library or book store.
- Read everywhere – even in the bath with plastic books.
- Let the one year-old turn pages of board and cloth books.
- End the activity by always saying "the end."

TWOS & THREES

- Point to printed words, identifying sounds and letter combinations.
- Select short, familiar themed stories with lots of illustrations.
- Re-read favorites many times.
- Use board books and sturdy Lift-Flap books.
- Storytellers often use felt boards with felt pieces to help tell a story.
- Finger puppets are especially nice to help imagine the story.
- Teach proper care of books; don't stand on them, read with clean hands, and do not eat or drink while reading, etc.

FOURS & FIVES

- Point out the upper and lower case letters.
- Read nursery rhymes, poems, and books of verse pausing to allow children to fill in rhyming words.
- Take children to meet their favorite traveling authors.
- Reading aloud helps advance attention spans and enriches the knowledge of literary topics and titles.
- Attend a costumed character story time.
- Use Lift-Flap books, Create-Your-Own Ending books, and Pop-Up books.
- Conduct a picture walk.
- Talk about the author and illustrator and compare stories he knows with the same author or illustrator.

SIX & BEYOND

- Have these children begin to write their own story.
- Discuss the four components of good literature: character, setting, problem, and solution.
- Visit a local printing company or copy shop to see how books can be created.
- Participate in reading programs that emphasize lots of reading time and learning new vocabulary words.
- Introduce different types of literature.
- Join a children's book club.
- Read chapter books, reference materials, magazines, television guide, cereal boxes, maps, etc.

Behind-the-Scenes tours are a great way to learn about how things work.

Behind-the-Scenes

"You have brains in your head; you have feet in your shoes. You can steer yourself in any direction you choose." – Dr Seuss

Behind-the-scenes tours are a unique way to further investigate routine locations and particular outing favorites while learning about how things work. When considering these types of outings, think about what your child does with you on weekly errand days and how you might incorporate these activities into a more in-depth understanding.

Most three year-olds know something about fire stations, fast food eateries and the local pizza restaurant. Four and five year-olds can handle more advanced tours including grocery stores, recycling centers, ice cream shops, and bakery companies. Six to ten year-olds will enjoy more complicated tours including banks/credit unions, places of worship, the dentist, and food manufacturers. Children aged eleven and older will appreciate tours that meet curriculum studies such as newspaper offices, car dealers, law enforcement, and medical facilities.

When deciding on a particular behind-the-scenes location, think about what you want your child to learn or experience and choose either a professionally led tour or one that you can narrate. For example, if your child is fascinated by kitchen creations from a favorite restaurant, a professional tour guided by a culinary employee is best. If there are opportunities for watching a particular process, such as donuts riding a conveyer belt on their way to being glazed, talk about this while watching together.

More tips to make professionally guided behind-the-scenes activities more successful:

- Most young children will not be patient for more than 30 minutes; avoid scheduling a tour that will require more time. Are you joining a group already scheduled that day?
- Ask if the script be geared to the age of the children in attendance?
- Ask when is the best time, or day, for the visit? If it is a restaurant, try to avoid the meal time hours, if it is April 15th; don't schedule a tour at the post office!

- Confirm complete directions and ask about any construction in the area and available parking.

- Upon completion of the tour, send a thank you note or email and if possible, have the children draw a picture or write the note personally. This almost guarantees you will get a positive nod when you call for a repeat tour.

Tips for successful "Mom" narrated or Self-Guided Tour:

- Watch for locations with large windows looking out onto a production floor (for example: donut shops or car dealers).

- Consider areas where people are moving with a purpose (Grocers stocking shelves or produce displays, floral arrangers, or bakery chefs).

- Look for unexpected places for great tours. Whenever you see a process in progress, stop and point out what is happening to your child. Ask questions about what your child sees and the possible outcome of the finished product.

Know Where to Go
Suggested Behind-the-Scenes Tours in DFW

American Airlines Center – Dallas
www.americanairlinescenter.com/guest-services/public_tours.php

Children's Medical Center – Dallas
www.childrens.com

Cowboy Stadium – Arlington
www.stadium.dallascowboys.com/tours/tourInfo_InfoTime.cfm

Environmental Discovery Center - Backyard Compost Demonstration Site – Plano - *Self-Guided
www.livegreeninplano.obsres.com

McDonald's – O'Reilly Group – locations around greater Collin County area
www.oreillymcd.com

Medical Center of Plano – Plano
www.themedicalcenterofplano.com

Mozzarella Cheese Company – Dallas - *Observation only, no tour
www.mozzco.com

Mrs. Baird's Bread – Fort Worth
www.mrsbairds.com

SeaLife Aquarium – Grapevine
www.visitsealife.com/Grapevine

Texas Motor Speedway – Fort Worth
www.texasmotorspeedway.com/at-track/speedway-facilities/track-tours

Texas Rangers Ballpark – Arlington
texas.rangers.mlb.com/tex/ballpark/tours/index.jsp

U.S. Bureau of Engraving & Printing Western Currency Facility – Fort Worth
www.moneyfactory.gov

Vetro Art – Grapevine - *Observation only, no tour
www.vetroartglass.com

Know Where to Go
Suggested Behind-the-Scenes Tours Beyond DFW

Blue Bell Ice Cream Factory Tour – Brenham, TX
www.bluebell.com

Collin Street Bakery – Corsicana, TX
www.collinstreet.com

Jardine Foods – Buda, TX - *Observation only, no tour
www.jardinefoods.com

Mary of Puddin' Hill – Greenville, TX - *Self-Guided
www.puddinhill.com

Nokona Athletic Goods Company - Nocona, TX
www.nokona.com

Pape's Pecan Company - Seguin, TX
www.papepecan.com

SAS Shoe Factory and General Store – San Antonio, TX
www.sasshoes.com

Southwest Dairy Museum - Sulphur Springs, TX - *Observation and exhibits
www.southwestdairyfarmers.com

Wimberley Glass Works - San Marcos, TX - *Observation only, no tour
www.wgw.com/about-wimberley-glassworks/demonstrations

What Your Kids Can Learn Here
Age Appropriate Activities for Behind-the-Scenes Tours

ONE YEAR OLDS

- Due to the nature of tours, we do not recommend taking this age on a tour unless this is part of a family outing.

TWOS & THREES

- Keep the tour short and operations highly visible.
- Talk them through each stage using simple vocabulary.
- Introduce process concepts: first, next, last.
- Fire stations and locations with trucks make good tours.

FOURS & FIVES

- Introduce vocabulary unique to the location.
- Tour should be a short walking distances with hands-on activities, if possible.
- Identify process concepts: beginning, middle, and end.
- Bakeries, recycling centers, grocery stores make great hands-on tours.

SIX & BEYOND

- Take these children on a variety of tours, which will offer more advanced hands-on and longer walking.
- Identify process concepts: first, second, third, last and results.
- At home, these children may be able to perform some of the steps to create what they viewed on tour. Try making a loaf of bread, rolling coins, etc.
- Consider post office, bank/credit union, hardware store, etc.

Consider asking a local bakery for a behind-the-scenes tour.

Behind-the-Scenes Featured Destinations

Blue Bell Ice Cream Factory Tour

Mary of Puddin' Hill

McDonald's

*U.S. Bureau of Engraving & Printing
Western Currency Facility*

Blue Bell Creamery

800-327-8135

1101 South Blue Bell Road, Brenham, TX

www.bluebell.com/the_little_creamery/visiting_blue_bell/VisitBB_Brenham.html

WHAT: Ice cream factory

HOURS: Mon - Fri @ 8:30am -3pm

ADMISSION: $6/Adults; $4/Kids 6-14 yrs

If you like ice cream, this is a must! And what a sweet treat it is! Ice cream lovers of all ages will definitely enjoy this tour. It will leave you wanting more and Blue Bell accommodates.

They live true to their motto, *"We eat all we can and sell the rest."* The tour guide informed us that they do indeed get to eat all they want when they are at work (on their break of course). While passing their break room, sure enough, we saw the freezers stocked with every kind of frozen treat they make. That is an ice cream lover's dream.

The factory tour lasts 45 minutes and to give you something to look forward to, everyone receives a FREE scoop of ice cream at the end of the tour. As you walk on elevated walkways you can look down through the large glass windows to see the ice cream being made. It is very interesting (and tormenting – "see but can't eat!") – especially for ice cream lovers.

TIPS FROM THE AROUND TOWN MOM

✓ *Amenities include: Restrooms and gift shop*

✓ *If you want more ice cream after your tour, it sells for only $1/ scoop.*

✓ *Tickets for the "day" go on sale at 8am on a first come, first served basis. This is a VERY popular tour. They only take 50 people per tour so factor that in to your departure plan.*

✓ *There are no restaurants close to the factory. If you drive down the "day of" like we did, plan on packing a lunch or include some time to stop along the way.*

ONE YEAR OLDS

- Due to the nature of tours, we do not recommend taking this age on a tour unless they are going along with the rest of the family.

TWOS & THREES

- In the lobby, ask: Can you find the horse in one of the photos?
- Talk them through each stage of making ice cream using simple vocabulary.
- Introduce process concepts of how ice cream is made: *first, next, last.*
- Count how many people are working.
- Obtain a paper ice cream hat from the ice cream shop area for your child and let them pretend to be an ice cream man.

FOURS & FIVES

- Discuss the ice cream making process concepts in terms of: *beginning, middle, and end.*
- Ask: What are the employees wearing that indicates they work in an ice cream factory?
- Using action words, talk about what the employees are doing.
- Discuss protective clothing the kitchen workers are wearing on their heads and bodies.
- At home collect the ice cream containers in the 1/2 gallon size and pint size for building and volume skills.

SIX & BEYOND

- In the lobby, view the vintage photos showing the history of Blue Bell and discuss the importance of horses for deliveries.
- Introduce vocabulary including: *creamery, flavorings, scooper, whisk.*
- Ask: How many flavors does Blue Bell offer? Which are the most popular? Which flavors are consumed by famous people?
- Find out how many different types of ice cream desserts Blue Bell makes.
- At home, make your own ice cream for the family using a crank or freezer style.

Mary of Puddin Hill

800-545-8889
201 E. Interstate 30 Exit 95, Greenville, TX
www.puddinhill.com

WHAT: Chocolate Confectionary and retail store

HOURS: Mon – Sat @ 9am – 6pm

ADMISSION: Free

Being a chocolate lover, I was thrilled to be here! Upon entering the retail store there are so many choices you hardly know what to choose first. The staff is happy to give out samples for your tasting pleasure.

I learned a lot by going here. Never having been a fan of brittle or toffee because it sticks to your teeth, I was pleasantly surprised to learn that theirs does not. And the reason why it doesn't? The owner was quick to educate me – it's because they use a higher grade butter and sugar. Who knew? I might love chocolate, but I don't manufacture it.

They make their own chocolate on the premises Monday through Friday. There are large glass windows you can peer into the manufacturing floor to see how they make the chocolate, decorate the candies and assemble them. Based on that, this is a "self-guided" tour that parents would need to talk their children through.

TIPS FROM THE AROUND TOWN MOM

✓ *Amenities include: Restrooms*

✓ *If there was something you wished you had purchased but did not, they have an online store. See their website.*

✓ *Holidays are a special time to visit as they have seasonal candies such as chocolate Easter Bunnies and Santas.*

✓ *Spring is an optimal time of year to visit as the bluebonnets and other wildflowers are in bloom. Take your kiddos' photos in the bluebonnets while out in Greenville.*

- Sense of smell will be highlighted at this location.
- Help your child identify different animals formed in chocolate.
- Allow your child a taste of sample candy.

TWOS & THREES

- Count the candies in a particular area or serving dish.
- Ask: How many pieces have the same shape or design?
- Sample the candy. Ask: Which is your favorite? Why?
- Identify the circular or square candies.
- Identify the shapes of boxes the candies are packaged in.

FOURS & FIVES

- Ask: Do you see more circular or square candies?
- At the long window, watch the confectioners make the candies.
- Ask: Is that mixer like ours at home?
- Introduce new vocabulary: *flavorings, extract, macaroon, toffee, apron.*
- Ask: What are the kitchen workers wearing on their heads and bodies?

SIX & BEYOND

- Ask: What tools are used to shape chocolates?
- Ask: What flavors do you think would go well with a chocolate candy?
- Discuss the process of making chocolate. Ask: What is the first step? What is the last step?
- Ask: Where does the candy go after they make it?
- At home, research the origins of chocolate and the importance of this non-sweet product to their culture.

McDonald's

972-985-8953
www.oreillymcd.com

WHAT: Fast-food hamburger restaurant

HOURS: By appointment

ADMISSION: Free

We have all heard of McDonald's and have been there some time in our lives whether it's for a burger or just a cup of coffee. McDonald's not only pioneered the fast-food concept, they were also the first to engage children whether it was by the introduction of characters such as Ronald McDonald, Happy Meals or their PlayLands. I don't know about you, but we spent many hours at their PlayLands when my son was younger.

You'll be happy to know that McDonald's can offer your children something more than a Happy Meal and time to play. A trip to McDonald's can also be very educational. O'Reilly McDonald's, a franchise group owned locally by the O'Reilly family, are happy to arrange free behind-the-scenes tours of their kitchen for your group. Call ahead to book your tour.

TIPS FROM THE AROUND TOWN MOM

✓ *Amenities include: Restrooms, restaurant*

✓ *Strollers are not permitted in the kitchen area on the tours.*

✓ *Children are not allowed to touch anything in the kitchen and are asked to keep their hands at their sides so they don't get hurt. If you think your child is too wiggly to follow this rule, this might not be the best tour.*

- Due to the nature of tours, we do not recommend taking this age on a tour unless they are going along with the rest of the family.

TWOS & THREES

- Stand in the freezer and feel how cold it is.
- Count how many people are working.
- Ask: What shape is a hamburger patty? A hamburger bun?
- Ask: Who are "Ronald McDonald" and the "Hamburglar"?

FOURS & FIVES

- If permitted, wave to the people in the drive-through lane.
- Point out the steps involved in making a cheeseburger/ hamburger.
- Using action words, talk about what the employees are doing.
- In the stockroom point out the large containers. Compare the large bottles of ketchup or huge sleeves of paper cups to the ones you have at home.
- Ask: How many French Fries are in the average small serving?

SIX & BEYOND

- Ask your tour guide why McDonald's chose the arches for their logo.
- Observe McDonald's innovation first hand – their automated drink dispenser. Ask: Does this help dispense drinks faster? More accurately?
- Point out the specially designed salt dispenser for salting French Fries and talk about how this helps ensure each batch of French Fries has the proper amount of salt.
- Notice the size of the sinks. Ask: Why is it important they are this size?
- Ask: Who was Ray Kroc and what contributions did he make to the food industry?

U.S. Bureau of Printing and Engraving

866-865-1194
9000 Blue Mound Road, Fort Worth, TX
www.moneyfactory.gov

WHAT: Western Currency Facility where currency is manufactured for the US Treasury Department

HOURS: Tues – Fri @ 8:30am - 5:30pm

ADMISSION: Free

Now you can really prove to your kids that "money doesn't grow on trees!" They can see with their own eyes how money really is made. As you walk along an enclosed walkway suspended over the production floor you can actually see billions of dollars being printed. One worker with a good sense of humor noticed everyone looking at a huge stack of bills at his work station. He held up a hand-written sign indicating there was $12 Million sitting right next to him. Wow!

Since tours are on a first come-first serve basis you may have to wait. Before or after your tour, enjoy two floors of interactive exhibits showcasing the history of currency and the intricacies of the printing process. Also be sure to check out the film.

It's really quite an honor that this facility is located in Texas. The facility in Washington DC, and this one in Ft. Worth are the only two facilities in the United States that print paper currency. Here's a tidbit: this is the only facility that prints the $2 bill. They are not as scarce as you would think, but many of us hold on to them anyway. As a result, they only need to print the $2 bill every 3 – 5 years.

TIPS FROM THE AROUND TOWN MOM
- ✓ *Amenities include: Restrooms, vending machines and gift shop*
- ✓ *No cameras or cell phones allowed, so leave them at home or in the car.*
- ✓ *You will have to go through a metal detector and security before entering the facility.*
- ✓ *This is a long ride for most of us and there aren't any restaurants at, or close to the facility. There are many places along the way on the many highways you will traverse to get there so you can eat before or after.*
- ✓ *The facility has a very informative FAQ page on their website geared towards older kids and adults. Check it out for some talking points.*

- A ride on the bus to the main facility is fun.
- Walking with the tour, talk about what the people are doing below.
- Wave at the workers and they will wave back!

TWOS & THREES

- The transfer station will interest this age as well as the main facility.
- Get a copy of the children's activity book from the front desk for use during and after the tour.
- Visit the museum upstairs.
- Look closely at the $20 under the magnifier. Ask: What shapes and designs do you see?
- On the tour, watch the men and women doing their jobs. Ask: What are they doing?

FOURS & FIVES

- In the children's activity book, turn to the center page and find the items on the one dollar bill.
- Talk about money as it relates to purchasing. Ask: How is money used?
- Explain that this facility makes bills, not coins. Ask: Which would you rather have – bills or coins? Why?
- The interactive museum will interest this age. Find the hands-on displays and discover new facts about making money.

SIX & BEYOND

- The children's activity book will challenge this age.
- Ask: What types of denominations are made at this facility?
- Define value and talk about how value is attributed to goods and services.
- Ask: How many colors are on the $20 bill? Can you name them?
- Ask: What is a watermark? Why is it important part of our bills?
- Ask: Where does the money go after it is made?

Understanding where food comes from and how it is prepared opens up new possibilities for your child to experience a greater food variety.

Food & Food Markets

"If you really want to make a friend, go to someone's house and eat with him... the people who give you their food give you their heart." – Cesar Chavez

Food is Power

One of the most difficult tasks of early parenting deals with food, specifically, how to get a child to eat healthy, well-balanced meals. This is complicated by the fact that children have their own ideas about food from early on. Between 18-24 months, children develop distinctive food preferences. Parenting magazines and pediatricians encourage offering a variety of foods to these children who will instinctively take in proper nutritional needs during this period.

With children two to seven years-old, eating becomes a more complex activity involving regulations and parental expectations (sit up at the table, use utensils, chew with your mouth closed, etc.). Again the advice is similar: keep a variety of foods on hand and don't expect terrific manners.

As children get older, eight years-old and older, it becomes increasingly more difficult to sit down together and eat. It has always been accepted that eating as a family five or more times a week produces "well-adjusted" teens. This is because eating together gives parents and children an opportunity to share the day's events, discuss challenges, and offer advice as well as fine tuning social skills and a child's sense of belonging. In addition, eating together encourages children to learn table manners, the art of conversation, memorize a blessing, and enhances their sense of humor.

In the next section you'll find a few food related activities that may make eating together more than fun as well as encourage kids to expand their personal menu. Understanding where food comes from, how it is prepared and different cultural feasting customs may make your mealtime experience a bit more interesting and create unique conversations.

Cultural markets offer teaching opportunities for new foods and exposure to new cultures.

Food & Food Markets:

SECTION I
Culturally Diverse
Neighborhood Markets

Touring culturally diverse corner markets can create discussions on people, families, cultures, and mealtime rituals. The variety of foods and flavors available for sampling and incorporating into the family diet are tremendous. If your selective eater does not appreciate white American rice, offer the Middle-Eastern style with orange curry and raisins. Your child might surprise you with his new palate! Within Dallas/Fort Worth look for the following:

Wet markets are those where live animals—most commonly the marine variety—are selected by the customer and slaughtered for the chosen parts. From the display case, children can identify the different parts of previously killed animals (pigs, chickens, cows, etc.) and watch live marine life swimming in tanks. Wet markets house packaged products and offer ready-to-eat foods which can be a good way to try a bite of something in its authentic delivery. Dry markets are similar except that animals/marine life are not slaughtered on the premises.

International grocery stores are great sensory adventures because they are often small and crowded with products. An authentic ethnic grocery store will usually have a small produce area; meat counter and seafood display along with canned, packaged, bottled and preserved goods. Household items such as dishware, cooking tools, religious artifacts, clothing, cleaners and gift items are commonly found. Many of these markets are owned and operated by families with young children on the premises.

Apparel markets, usually located within walking distance to international grocery stores, offer clothing, jewelry, cosmetics, shoes and other items for personal use. Purchasing a few items; reading materials, music, decorative items and religious artifacts can help re-create specific cultural ambiance in your home to enhance the mealtime experience.

Restaurants can either be the first step or a later step in a culturally diverse food adventure. You may sample specific foods at a restaurant before purchasing a take-home to cook version. Restaurants allow you to eat foods prepared authentically along with the right sauces, temperatures, beverages and condiments.

Because Dallas/Fort Worth is very culturally diverse, you might only have to go to the closest shopping center to find diverse cultural offerings. Neighborhoods where Middle Easterners, Indian/Pakistanis, Asians, and Mexicans dwell are fairly well known and are easy to find.

What Your Kids Can Learn Here
Age Appropriate Activities for Culturally Diverse Markets

ONE YEAR OLDS

At the market:

- Maneuver through the aisles and pathways.

- Watch faces and listen to voices.

- Tasting is important and water will help wash down flavors. Ask: Which flavors are most appealing? Which are not?

- Surrounding conversation and music may catch these children's attention.

In a restaurant:

- Place your child directly up to the table where she can hear and see everything going on.

- Offer numerous flavors and textures.

TWOS & THREES

At the market:

- Listen to voices, music and the sounds of the market business.

- Talk about produce and identify a few.

- Watch the live marine animals in the tanks and those live in boxes.

- Select a fruit, vegetable or starch to try at home.

In a restaurant:

- Allow discreet "playing" with their food to feel its texture.

- Ask: Is the table setting the same or different from home?

- Introduce new vocabulary words including the utensils used and the names of dishes being served.

FOURS & FIVES

At the market:

- Talk about the cultural housewares and clothing found at the market.

- Introduce new produce and products to these children.

- Choose a few foods to sample either at the market or at home. Ask: Which foods might go together to make a meal?

- Compare the market visited to other markets of the same or different culture.

In a restaurant:

- Talk about the food properties: sweet, sour, hard, soft, long, short, chewy, etc.
- Practice with special utensils.
- Watch the people in the restaurant. Ask: What are they doing? What are they saying?
- Observe written language on menus and art works hanging on the walls.
- Listen to the music overhead. Ask: What instruments do you hear?

SIX & BEYOND

At the market:

- Identify similar products found in many different cultures.
- Compare product labels written in different languages. Ask: Can you find a box of Kraft Macaroni & Cheese in another culture's language?
- Find clothing of the culture and dress up to represent a favorite nationality.
- Create your own country, its rules, colors, motto and customs.

In a *restaurant*:

- Try reading the menu.
- Ask: Can you identify a special group of symbols or characters that refer to "rice" or vegetables?
- Every culture in the world shares a specific food. Ask: What is it?
- Try to place your order in the native language.
- While at the restaurant, take note of customs and cooking dishes used to prepare the meal.

Food & Food Markets:

SECTION II
Farmers Markets

Consider visiting a farmers market or a "pick-your-own" location for an amazing lesson in many things edible. At both places you can purchase food that is fresher than what you can get in your local grocery store.

The concept of the local farmers market has been around for centuries. Some of the best known markets are in Africa, the Middle East and Europe and often depicted in Hollywood films and stories. Look closely at a map of our D/FW metroplex and you will find numerous references to the farm to market roads (FM) used by early regional farmers of the Blackland Prairie. In other states, these roads may be referred to as "CR" (country to railroad) or "GT" (garden to town).

Farmers markets, both American and mixed ethnic ones, may offer a huge display of products not limited to fruits and vegetables. Open seasonally, usually between April and October, these locations offer young children opportunities to see some familiar produce and introduces them to some unfamiliar products. The key to a good adventure is sampling, so encourage your children to taste and discover new favorites.

Similarly, "pick-your-own" activities can enhance your family meal experience by involving the children in selecting, cleaning and possibly preparing foods for the table. During this activity, children can learn how their favorite fruit or vegetable is planted, cultivated, and harvested. Go early in the day and remember to take sun screen and other hot weather precautions. Bring several sized buckets, gloves, newspapers to keep your vehicle clean and a wagon for the children to ride in.

Because our climate can be harsh on these growing facilities (lack of rain fall or natural destructive activities) and each season can bring new locations, contact the Texas Department of Agriculture at 512-463-7476 or for locations within the United States try *www.pickyourown.org* for a list of current places for this experience.

Know Where to Go
Suggested Farmers Markets in DFW

Coppell Farmers Market
www.coppellfarmersmarket.org

Dallas Farmers Market
www.dallasfarmersmarket.org

Denison Farmers Market
www.downtowndenisonfarmersmarket.com

Denton County Farmers Market
www.dentonfarmersmarket.com

Fort Worth Cowtown Market
www.ourfortworth.com/farmers_market/farmers_index.htm

Frisco Farmers Market
www.friscofarmersmarket.org

Grand Prairie Farmers Market
www.gptx.org/farmersmarket

Grapevine Farmers Market
www.farmersmarketofgrapevine.com

McKinney Farmers Market at Chestnut Square Historic Village and Adriatica
www.chestnutsquare.org/programs/farmers_market.asp

Plano Farmers Market at Fairview Farms
www.fairview-farms.com/farmers-market.html

What Your Kids Can Learn Here
Age Appropriate Activities for Farmers Markets & Pick-Your-Own

Farmers markets:

- Introduce colors and shapes of fruits and vegetables.
- Listen to people talk with one another and watch the many faces that come to buy produce.
- Try sampling some foods—what a treat!

Pick-your-own:

- Nothing like an outdoor stroll to get those lungs and leg muscles strong.
- Talk about the produce you see and its colors.
- Feel the textures of the product skins and stems.
- Be sure to sample after you purchase your pickings.

Farmers markets:

- Identify different shapes and sizes of produce.
- Notice subtle color differences among fruits and vegetables.
- Smell and taste a new food. Talk about how it tastes, feels in the mouth.
- Introduce new vocabulary: *aftertaste, spicy, sour.*
- Discuss their reactions to the new foods. Ask: Does it taste good?
- Ask: How can this food be served—with sugar? Between bread? Cooked?

Pick-your-own:

- Ask: Is the produce growing from a stem or vine? Find other produce growing differently.
- Begin to pick from the plant. Ask: Does it come off easily or do you need to pull hard?
- Show these children how to gently lay produce in the bucket to avoid squashing and damage.
- Talk about the proper way to clean fruit before sampling.

Farmers market:

- Identify fruit and vegetable medleys, Ask: What is summer squash, winter squash? Find different apple varieties, etc.
- Make a list of the foods found at the market.
- Talk about the different jobs offered at the market.
- Ask: Who is buying and who is selling?

Pick-your-own:

- Talk about the root systems. Ask: Are the roots raised or imbedded?
- Ask: How is irrigation accomplished? Are there visible hoses?
- Identify leaves associated with a particular plant. Pay special attention to how the produce hangs from the stem or vine.
- Discuss what you will do with the produce when you are home - bake a pie? Steam as a side dish to dinner? Make into a jam or preserves?
- Wash your fruits and vegetables before sampling!

SIX & BEYOND

Farmers market:

- Introduce new vocabulary: *vendor, customer, market, dealer.*
- Discover what non-food products are sold at the farmers market.
- Choose a recipe you wish to make and find your ingredients at the farmers market.
- Notice the money exchanging hands. Ask: Are all the vendors charging the same price for the same products?
- Ask: What parts of the world do products come from?

Pick-your-own:

- Talk about the types of tools farmers use to plant and harvest their fields.
- Many farmers are leaving the fields to work at different jobs. Ask: How will this affect our food supply?
- Discuss migrant farm labor role in large farms.
- Ask: How does weather play a role in farming?
- Try growing a fruit or vegetable garden at home.

Historic Museums & Sites

Historic sites and cultural museums offer children valuable concepts including the passage of time and their placement in the family. The idea of "a long time ago" is difficult for children to understand because young children cannot comprehend anyone having a life before they were born. In addition, these same children often see their place as the center of the family universe with everything rotating around their needs and wants.

Visiting historic sites serves to introduce artifacts that show time before they were born allowing them to visualize their role in a family of an unknown period. Some of our best locations offer children artifacts to manipulate, period costumes to don, experience specific age-appropriate chores, and think about how they may have spent their time " a long time ago". Bring grandparents to add a personal lesson as older generations tell their stories and share remembrances.

History teaches children about the passage of time as well as our nation's traditions, conflicts, ideas and values.

Know Where to Go
Suggested Historic Museums & Sites in DFW

African American Museum – Denton
*www.discoverdenton.com/play.
cfm?l=146&b=144*

Allen Heritage Center & Museum -
Allen
www.allemheritage.org

A.W. Perry Homestead Museum -
Carrollton
www.cityofcarrollton.com/museum

Ball-Eddleman-McFarland House –
Fort Worth
*www.historicfortworth.org/Weddings
Tours/BallEddlemanMcFarland
House/tabid/376/Default.aspx*

Bayless-Selby House – Denton
*www.dentonwiki.org/Bayless-
Selby_House_Museum*

Chestnut Square Historical Village –
McKinney
www.chestnutsquare.org

Dallas Heritage Village - Dallas
www.dallasheritagevillage.org

**Eisenhower Birthplace State
Historical Museum** - Denison
*www.visiteisenhowerbirthplace.com/
index.aspx?page=5*

Farmers Branch Historical Park -
Farmers Branch
www.farmersbranch.info

Fielder House Museum – Arlington
www.arlingtontxhistoricalsociety.org

Florence Ranch Homestead –
Mesquite
www.cityofmesquite.com

Frisco Heritage Museum - Frisco
www.friscomuseum.com

Grapevine Heritage Center – Grapevine
*www.grapevinetexasusa.com/
Default.aspx?TabId=529*

Heard Craig Historical Center –
McKinney
www.heardcraig.org

Heritage Farmstead Museum - Plano
www.heritagefarmstead.org

Irving Heritage House – Irving
www.irvingheritage.com/

**Jackie Townsell Bear Creek Heritage
Museum** - Irving
*www.irvingtexas.com/listings/
Jackie-Townsell-Bear-Creek-
Heritage-Center/781*

Knapp Heritage Park - Arlington
*www.historicalarlington.org/knapp_
heritage_park.html*

Little Chapel-in-the-Woods – Denton
www.twu.edu

Log Cabin Village - Fort Worth
www.logcabinvillage.org

Nash Farm - Grapevine
*www.grapevinetexasusa.com/
Heritage/NashFarm/tabid/522/
Default.aspx*

Old City Cemetery – Plano
www.chancy.org

Old Red Courthouse – Dallas
www.oldred.org

**Penn Farms Agricultural History
Center** – Cedar Hill
*www.tpwd.state.tx.us/publications/
pwdpubs/media/pwd_br_4503
_0131o.pdf*

**Rockwall County Historical
Foundation Museum** – Rockwall
*www.rockwallcountyhistorical
foundation.com*

Thistle Hill - Fort Worth
www.historicfortworth.org

What Your Kids Can Learn Here
Age Appropriate Activities for Historic Museums & Sites

ONE YEAR OLDS

- Practice gross motor skills on different surfaces: gravel, brick, stone, wood plants, stairs, dirt.
- Listen to the sounds you hear.
- Touch equipment and artifacts on display outside.
- Visit with animals, if available.
- Identify simple artifacts.

TWOS & THREES

- Find the kitchen, family room, bed room(s).
- Find different colors and shapes.
- Look for collections of specific artifacts and compare them within the group.
- Use concepts of big/bigger and small/smaller when comparing size of the dwelling and out-buildings.
- Discuss how many people lived in the house and what they may have done for a living.

FOURS & FIVES

- Compare artifacts at this site with those found in your house.
- Ask: What crops were planted on the property?
- Ask: What tools were used to plant and harvest these crops?
- Talk about the types of chores a child might have to perform as part of this family. Ask: Do you do the same chores at home?
- Ask: What materials were used to build the house, barns and other out-buildings?
- Find patterns throughout the site.
- Role play in the special reproduction buildings/rooms.
- Ask: How was communication with the outside world performed?
- Identify the out-buildings by their function.
- Ask: What role did neighbors play in the community?
- Ask: How were holidays celebrated?
- Find evidence of recycling.
- Ask: What did pioneer people do for recreation?

- Talk about the history of the community.
- Ask: How did the inhabitants make a living?
- Learn about the processes used in food preservation: canning, curing, smoking, baking, etc.
- Talk about technology advancements which made pioneer life easier.
- New vocabulary: *parlor, ice box, coffee grinder, hair wreath, cistern*
- Watch videos provided by the site.
- Look for secret rooms, staircases, passageways and pocket doors.
- Ask: Where does the water supply come from?
- Identify family photographs hanging in the house – talk about clothing, hair styles and fashion of the period.
- Ask: How did information reach people living apart?
- Discuss different types of chores and who was responsible for tending to them.
- Talk about transportation. Ask: How were goods and services transported?

Historic Museums & Sites Featured Destinations

Dallas Heritage Village

Eisenhower Birth Place State Historical Museum

Frisco Heritage Museum

Heritage Farmstead Museum

Log Cabin Village

Dallas Heritage Village

214-421-5141
1515 South Harwood Street, Dallas, TX
www.dallasheritagevillage.org

WHAT: 1840-1910 historic building complex

HOURS: Tues – Sat @ 10am – 4pm; Sun @ 12pm – 4pm; Closed Mondays

ADMISSION: $9/Adults; $7/Seniors; $5/Children ages 4-12; Under 4 yrs - Free

Nestled within the Dallas city limits on 20 wooded acres, this historic site features 38 Victorian and pioneer buildings for both active and restful learning. Formerly known as Old City Park because this was the site of Dallas' first city park, Dallas Heritage Village is maintained by the City of Dallas and is part of the DISD curriculum.

This is a great place to educate children about nineteenth century life. Kids won't be so squeamish about going to the dentist after they see what this dentist's office looked like. Stop in the General Store so kids can see how people did their grocery shopping in the nineteenth century before Kroger and Target.

TIPS FROM THE AROUND TOWN MOM

✓ *Amenities include: Restrooms and water fountains, Snacks and drinks available for purchase in the ticket office.*

✓ *Pack a picnic, lots of old shady trees around for coverage.*

✓ *Kids are free on the third Sunday of the month.*

✓ *Dallas Heritage Village offers many events throughout the year so be sure to check their website or the AroundTownKids event calendar: www.AroundTownKidsFrisco.com/events.htm*

✓ *Audio tours enable you to hear the history of the buildings as well as first-person interpretations through your cell phone.*

- This large sprawling area allows for stretching the legs and tumbling down the hills in the center of the park.
- Walk the cobblestone walkway on Main Street.
- Enjoy an active game of "peek-a-boo" at the teepee.
- Point out the different buildings by name: teepee, Victorian home, dogtrot house, store, etc.

TWOS & THREES

- Visit the teepee, gazebo, dog-trot house, potter's workshop, church and log cabin.
- Find the vegetables and herb garden, meet the small farm animals.
- During shearing season, watch the sheep being sheared and wool spun into thread.
- Identify shapes seen in the building's architecture.
- Play "I Spy" with colors, objects, and letters.

FOURS & FIVES

- Talk about the function of other buildings on this site including the antebellum mansion, potter's workshop, school, curing shed and train depot. Ask: How did these buildings help this community thrive?
- Visit the working blacksmiths and see how horseshoes and nails are struck.
- Visit the garden. Ask: Which plants can you identify?
- While visiting the homes, ask: Can you find a bathroom? If no, why not?

SIX & BEYOND

- Talk about the needs of a community and how this site offered a good place for pioneers to settle.
- The general store offers a myriad of interesting toys and tools for an up-close observation.
- Find out how the "Shotgun House" got its name.
- Experience a bit of history on this outing with a tour offered by costumed docents.
- At home, build your own pioneer town out of sugar cubes, cereal boxes and paper towel tubes.

Eisenhower Birth Place
State Historical Museum

903-465-8908
609 S. Lamar Ave, Denison, TX
www.visiteisenhowerbirthplace.com

WHAT: Modest two-story frame house birthplace of our 34th president, Dwight D. Eisenhower, and museum.

HOURS: Tues–Sat @ 9am – 5pm; Sun @ 1pm –5pm

ADMISSION: $4/Adults; $3/Ages 6-18/Students; 5 and under - Free

Although Dwight D. Eisenhower did not grow up in Texas, we can claim him as having been born in our state. Since only two US Presidents were born in Texas, it is fortunate for us that one of them was born just up the road, so to speak. What better way to introduce children to great men in history and the office of the US Presidency than visiting a president's home?

Be sure to stop in the museum in addition to the home to view many historical artifacts relating to Eisenhower's presidency as well as the era. Who knew Eisenhower was an artist? The museum has copies of several of his paintings as well as one original.

TIPS FROM THE AROUND TOWN MOM

✓ *Amenities include: Restrooms, water fountains and gift shop*

✓ *There is no food available for purchase. There are picnic tables and shady areas to enjoy the picnic or food you brought from home.*

- This age group will enjoy running and walking in the spacious grassy area.
- Point out the large features of this site using vocabulary including the statue, farmhouse, railroad tracks, and bridge.

- In the house, ask: Can you find the baby shoes?
- Point out the baby cradle and ask: Who slept in this small bed?
- Count how many windows are in the front of the house.
- In the dining room, talk about the shape of the plates and other objects.
- Ask: If you lived here, which room would you play in?

- In the museum, talk about the clothing worn in the historical photographs.
- In the house, see how many toys your child can identify in the parlor.
  - Ask: Do you see a TV in the parlor? Why not?
  - Ask: What do you see in the kitchen that we have in our home today?
- Visit the herb garden and identify what plants are growing during your visit. Talk about the importance of a garden to families.

- In the museum, find the campaign buttons on display. Ask: How were these used and for what purpose?
  - Watch the 12 minute informational video.
- In the house, ask: What kinds of activities would the family have enjoyed in the parlor? Are those the same activities we would engage in today? What did they do for entertainment back then?
  - Note the stove in the parlor. Ask: Why is it in the parlor? What was it used for?
  - Point out that the doors and windows were opposite from each other and explain the concept of cross-ventilation.
- Outside the house, view the railroad tracks. Observe the end of the tracks and the remaining built up area where the tracks used to run. Ask: Why do the tracks end?

Frisco Heritage Museum

972-292-5665
6455 Page Street, Frisco, TX
www.friscomuseum.com

WHAT: Dozens of rare artifacts and photographs depicting Frisco's past from a small farming town to one of the fastest growing cities in the country.

HOURS: Wed-Sat @ 10am-5pm; Sun @ 1pm-5pm; Closed Mon & Tues

ADMISSION: $4/Adults; $3/Seniors; $2/Kids 5-11 yrs; 4 & under - Free; $8/Family

Many of you may recognize this place as it is next to Babe's Chicken as well as being a great photography spot with all of its vintage out-buildings. Some of you may have even had your family photo taken here.

This museum is quite a treasure trove of local history and a wonderful place to start educating your children on the more recent past, especially if you live in the area. You or your parents may get your own "blast from the past" seeing the "den" set up from the 1960s. If your parents or grandparents are in town they might enjoy visiting this museum with you and make the history come alive for you and your children.

Be sure to take a moment to admire and discuss the covered wagon in the lobby. Also notice the mural. The staff told me it was painted by an artist and shipped to the museum in pieces for installation. You would never know it by looking at it.

TIPS FROM THE AROUND TOWN MOM

✓ *Amenities include: Restrooms, water fountains and a gift shop with many reasonably priced educational and historical reproduction toys.*

✓ *Frisco Heritage Museum offers regular events so stay tuned to their website or the AroundTownKids calendar: www.AroundTownKidsFrisco.com/events.htm*

✓ *The out-buildings are open for exploration from 1:00-4:00 p.m. on the third Sunday of each month.*

- Upstairs, visit the "Children's Area." Touch the artifacts on display as part of the Blackland Prairie exhibit.
- Identify several of the artifacts by name and show the one-year old how they are used.
- Emulate the animal noises that a live chicken, sheep, cow make.

TWOS & THREES

- Find the fire truck and antique cars.
- Find the Coca-Cola bottles on display and count them.
- In the Children's Area, ask: Can you count the eggs? Can you count the quilts?
  - Name the animals upstairs on display.
  - Put the vegetables in the buckets.
  - Touch the cotton on display. Ask: How does it feel?

FOURS & FIVES

- In the Children's Area, talk about the types of chores a child might have to perform as part of this pioneer family and compare these chores with those you do today. Pretend to wash the clothes using the wash board.
- Find artifacts that are similar and different to those found in your house.
- Ask: Can you find the telephones?
- Notice the covered wagon in the lobby. Discuss this as a form of pioneer transportation. Ask: Do you think the ride was comfortable? Was it bumpy?
- Ask: What did pioneer people do for recreation? Can you find the checker board?

SIX & BEYOND

- Learn about the processes used in food preparation in the kitchen exhibit and how things have changed since the days of the beauty parlor on display. Ask: Can you find the hair curlers?
- Talk about technology advancements which made pioneer life easier.
- Watch the videos in the upstairs movie theater.
- Talk about transportation – how were goods and services transported?
- Ask: Can you find the TV remote in the 1960s den?

Heritage Farmstead Museum

972-881-0140
1900 West 15th Street, Plano, TX
www.heritagefarmstead.org

WHAT: Four acre complex with an historic home, gardens, a windmill, animals and 12 original out buildings.

HOURS: Tues – Sun @ 10am - 4:30 pm

ADMISSION: *Self-Guided Tours:* $2/Person; 3 & under - Free; *Docent Tours:* $5/Adults;$3.50/Seniors and children 4-18; 3 & under - Free

This historic complex is an excellent example of life on the Blackland Prairie located in the midst of Plano. Although the large Victorian home is definitely the showpiece, one of the most interesting features is the reproduction one-room schoolhouse. The key word being "reproduction" – children can touch and feel all that is displayed within the school.

There is so much to see and do here and lots of open spaces for younger ones to run around. The Farmstead has many community and seasonal events and ongoing programs so be sure to check their website or the AroundTownKids event calendar: *www.AroundTownKidsPlano.com/events.htm*

TIPS FROM THE AROUND TOWN MOM

✓ *Amenities include: Restrooms and water fountain*

✓ *The grounds can be muddy after the rain and strollers might be hard to push on the gravel walkways.*

✓ *Bring bug spray if you wander down to the creek.*

In the main house:
- Identify the rooms by name.
- Point out larger artifacts such as the stove, trunks, and beds.

Outside:
- Walk to the chicken coop to see live chickens.
- Ring the school bell.
- Identify the animals on site and emulate their sounds.

TWOS & THREES

In the main house:
- Introduce new vocabulary words: *bonnet, tin ear, well.*
- Ask: Can you identify the sofa, lamp, books, instruments, shoes, or blocks?

Outside:
- Visit the one room schoolhouse and play school.
- Attend a special pre-school program.
- If accompanied by a docent, touch the animals.

FOURS & FIVES

In the main house:
- Ask: What is the "tin ear" and how does it work?
- Ask: Can you find the tiny play stove? The hair wreath? The ice box?
- Introduce new vocabulary words including *mill, sorghum,* and *chamber pot.*
- Ask: How does a butter churn work?

Outside:
- Talk about the purpose of the root cellar.
- Visit the one room schoolhouse and role play.
- Go inside the Pole barn and see what is stored inside.

SIX & BEYOND

In the main house:
- Find the sleeping porch and learn about its purposes.
- Ask: What is a transom and how does it work?
- Ask: Who lived in this house and what was her passion?

Outside:
- Ask: How is the main house, built by Hunter Farrell, different from the Young House or the share croppers dwelling?
- Ask: What is the difference between a cistern and a well?
- Find three tools on the site that are different from tools we use today for the same purpose.

Log Cabin Village

817-392-5881
2100 Log Cabin Village Lane, Fort Worth TX
www.logcabinvillage.org

WHAT: Historic structures, furnished with authentic artifacts, provides a vivid look at life in the nineteenth century North Texas frontier (1840-1890).

HOURS: Tue-Fri @ 9am-4pm; Sat & Sun @ 1-5pm

ADMISSION: $5/Adults; $4.50/Seniors & 4-17 yrs; under 3 – free

We like this village with its water wheel and log cabin houses. Each one holds something special to learn about. Watch the blacksmith make horseshoes and other iron tools, while the candle maker dips wicks into hot wax the old fashioned way.

Don't miss the Pioneer Herb Garden, well-maintained herb plants established in 1992 by the Fort Worth Herb Society. Here you will find a demonstration garden consisting of 4 raised beds offering native Texas plants and herbs used by pioneer settlers for culinary and medicinal purposes.

This village is a nice area to walk around, lots of trees and scenery. Pack a picnic lunch, as just across the village is a large semi-wooded area to run and have lunch on picnic tables.

TIPS FROM THE AROUND TOWN MOM

✓ *Amenities include: Restrooms, gift shop with "old timey" items for sale including historic replicas and village made crafts.*

✓ *There are no snacks or drinks available for sale except a limited old-fashioned candy selection in the gift shop.*

- With the tinkering of the blacksmith's hammer, and the splashing of the water wheel from the gristmill, the one-year-old will hear some different sounds.
- This is a place for him to walk and try his balance over several small bridges.

TWOS & THREES

- Watch the blacksmith who may make a simple iron trinket—a nail or horseshoe. Ring the metal triangle bell.
- The candle maker will show children how to dip the strings into hot wax.
- Visit the one room schoolhouse and play school.
- Try on the straw hats, bonnets and prairie clothes.
- Manipulate the plastic eggs and chickens found in the chicken coop.

FOURS & FIVES

- Walk to the small mill wheel. Ask: How did the mill work and what was it used for?
- In the herb garden, find plants for healing and flavoring.
- At the one room schoolhouse, write your name on the individual blackboard slates.
- Have your child try to pump some water out of the well.
- Allow your child to grind some seeds.

SIX & BEYOND

- Visit the old school house and find the schoolmaster's home above the schoolroom. Ask: Why did the school master live here? Why was the school so small?
- Talk about the clothing worn by the costumed docents. Ask: Why were the styles so different from today?
- Discuss pioneer life in rural Texas. Ask: If you could go back in time, what career would you like to have? Why?
- Ask: What was the smokehouse used for?
- Ask: What foods did pioneers eat?

Nature Trails & Flower Gardens

Activities involving the exploration of nature trails and strolling through flower gardens are a favorite family adventure. Not only do these adventures provide educational studies but they also allow us to relax and forget the chores and homework waiting at home. Natural areas provide a variety of concepts to investigate - wildlife, topography, plants, insects, water flow, and urban planning.

Bring old sneakers or boots as creeks abound; and speaking of water - do not limit your outing to just sunny days. Discovering nature in the rain will be remembered for a long time. The plant world looks very different during a shower and creeks are there for getting wet.

When out in nature, all of a child's senses are activated allowing him to de-focus. As he becomes immersed in something bigger than himself it rejuvenates his brain.

Know Where to Go
Suggested Nature Trails & Flower Gardens

Arbor Hills Nature Preserve – Plano
www.planoparksandrecreation.com

Cedar Hill State Park – Cedar Hill
www.cedarhillstatepark.org

Cedar Ridge Preserve (formerly known as Dallas Nature Center) – Dallas
www.dallasparks.org

Celestial Park – Addison
www.addisontx.gov

Crape Myrtle Trails – McKinney
www.crapemyrtletrails.org

Dallas Arboretum & Botanical Garden – Dallas
www.dallasarboretum.org

Day Spring Nature Preserve – Allen
www.cityofallen.org

Dinosaur Valley State Park – Glen Rose
www.tpwd.state.tx.us/state-parks/dinosaur-valley

East Dallas Community Gardens – Dallas
www.gardendallas.org/east_dallas_community_garden.htm

Elm Fork Nature Preserve - Carrollton
www.cityofcarollton.com

Fort Worth Botanic Gardens & Conservatory – Fort Worth
www.fwbg.org

Fort Worth Nature Center & Refuge – Fort Worth
www.fwnaturecenter.org

Frisco Commons – Frisco
www.friscofun.org/parks

Grapevine Botanical Gardens - Grapevine
www.grapevinetexas.gov/facilities.aspx?page=detail&rid=6

Heard Natural Science Museum & Wildlife Sanctuary - McKinney
www.heardmuseum.org

Japanese Gardens - Oak Cliff, Dallas
www.friendsofoakcliffparks.org

Katy Trail – Dallas
www.katytraildallas.org

Lake Shore Trails – Flower Mound
www.trails.com

Lavender Ridge Farms – Gainesville - Pick your own lavender and herbs – call ahead for picking conditions
www.lavenderridgefarms.com

Nature Study and Hiking in North Central Texas – list of trails in the area
www.nhnet.org/nature/nature.htnl

Reverchon Park – Dallas
www.reverchonparkfriends.com

River Legacy Park – Arlington
www.riverlegacy.org

Shawnee Trail – Frisco
www.friscofun.org/parks/parks/Pages/ShawneeTrailSportsComplex.aspx

Spring Creek Nature Park - Richardson
www.cor.net

Sun Creek – Allen
www.active.com

Texas Discovery Gardens - Fair Park, Dallas
www.texasdiscoverygardens.org

What Your Kids Can Learn Here
Age Appropriate Activities for Nature Trails & Flower Gardens

ONE YEAR OLDS

Along the walk:
- Listen for birds, wolves, cars, trains
- "Look up, Look down, look all around".
- Take a stroll through nature.
- Hug a tree!

At the creek:
- Touch the water. Ask: How does it feel?
- Walk in the creek.

In the garden:
- Feel the weather on your face: warm sun, cool breeze, wet rain.
- Smell the flowers.
- Gently touch the petals.
- Watch the butterflies and other insects. Ask: Where are they going?

TWOS & THREES

Along the walk:
- Identify different trees and leaves.
- Notice how the trees are growing: straight up/bending sideways.
- Play "Follow-the-Leader".
- Make a tree rubbing.

At the creek:
- Walk a short distance in the creek.
- Ask: Can you find fish or tadpoles?
- Create an art project using natural resources found at the creek.

In the garden:
- Identify different flowers and plants.
- Find bugs and insects.
- Watch for sculpture.
- Visit the Nature Center, if available.

FOURS & FIVES

Along the walk:
- Wear a pedometer on your walk and see how many steps you can go.
- Use a compass and learn cardinal directions.
- Identify animals that live inside tree trunks and within the branches.

- Learn to identify poison ivy.
- Talk about "flying" seeds: *whirly-birds, parachute, etc.*
- Ask: Can you find mushrooms?
- Try reading the directional and informational signs.

At the creek:

- Look for fossils.
- Ask: What rocks can you identify?

In the garden:

- Ask: Why do some flowering plants have thorns?
- Ask: Why are colors important for flowers?
- Visit the Nature Center, if available

SIX & BEYOND

Along the walk:

- Identify direction in the woods.
- Calculate yards/miles walked.
- Talk about the topography.
- Discuss the reasons for knots on the tree limbs.
- Ask: What causes trees to split?
- Ask: Why does a tree drop its leaves?
- Ask: How does a tree protect the wildlife?
- Follow a pre-existing map on a hike.

At the creek:

- Ask: Where does the water come from?
- Ask: What evidence of erosion do you see?
- Talk about the different types of animals that live in a pond versus a stream.

In the garden:

- Ask: What tools are used to cultivate growing plants?
- Ask: How does sunlight play an important role in growing plants?
- Ask: What is photosynthesis? How does it work?
- Ask: Which insects are good for gardens?

At home:

- Plant your own garden using a container, soil, and seeds.
- Read books about nature, weather, faeries, rocks, and minerals.
- Learn the difference between man-made and natural habitats.

Nature Trails & Flower Gardens Featured Destinations

Dallas Arboretum & Botanical Garden

Dinosaur Valley State Park

Fort Worth Botanic Gardens

Grapevine Botanical Gardens

Heard Natural Science Museum & Wildlife Sanctuary

Dallas Arboretum and Botanical Garden

214-515-6500
8525 Garland Road, Dallas, TX
www.dallasarboretum.org

WHAT: 66 acres of flowers and display gardens

HOURS: Open daily 9am – 5pm; Closed Thanksgiving Day, Christmas Day and New Years Day.

ADMISSION: $15/Adults; $12/Seniors; $10/Children 3 - 12 yrs; Under 3 yrs – Free; Add $3/person for the Rory Meyers Gardens; $10/Parking

The Dallas Arboretum continues to expand its gardens and exhibits with great enthusiasm. This amazing oasis in southeastern Dallas reflects all that is beautiful and natural in North Texas. Meticulously maintained, the garden areas surround the DeGolyer Home; a Spanish style single story home built for Everette and Nell DeGolyer and their four children.

Throughout the year, the Dallas Arboretum kicks-off several seasons with special floral and colorful exhibits that are both beautiful and amazing. "Autumn at the Arboretum" with the spectacular Pumpkin Village is a "must-see." In addition, musical and theatrical performances are scheduled for audiences of all ages.

The Dallas Arboretum's newest achievement is the Rory Meyer's Children's Adventure Garden. We cannot address every wonderful attribute this new area offers but this is a must see for all ages. Using state-of-the-art technology in conjunction with natural resources, the exhibits cover many disciplines including math, energy sources, basic science, ecology, art, pre-history, architecture, and plant biology. This experience is best with an adult to guide and direct attentions.

TIPS FROM THE AROUND TOWN MOM

✓ *Amenities include: Restrooms, water fountains, restaurants and gift shop.*

✓ *Consider a membership to allow for multiple visits during the year and discounts for many of the activities.*

✓ *Bring your camera and pack a lunch. There are tables, as well as plenty of shady and grassy areas that are perfect for a picnic blanket.*

- Touch the plant leaves, rocks, and sculptures and describe the feel.
- Listen to birds, waterfalls, and voices.

At the Rory Meyer's Children Adventure Garden:

- Walk through the *Dripping Springs Trail* and listen to recordings of specific bird calls.
- Play in the water in the *Entry Plaza* area and visit the *First Adventure* area.

- Watch for butterflies, birds, squirrels, and fish.
- Find the sculpture "Thank Heaven for Little Girls" in the small garden area outside the DeGolyer Home.

At the Rory Meyer's Children Adventure Garden:

- At the *Moody Oasis* area, talk about the colors and different shapes of the flowers and plants.
- In the *Amazing Secret Garden*, find your way through the maze.

- At the *Women's Gardens* talk about the purpose of a reflecting pool. Ask: How deep is the water?
- Using paper and crayons, make rubbings of the variety of textured surfaces.
- Find the four spitting frogs sculpture and explore the water.

At the Rory Meyer's Children Adventure Garden:

- In the *Life Cycles* area, learn to tell time with the human sun dial and participate in the hands-on activities at the flowing river exhibit.
- In the *Kaleidoscope* area, design a garden landscape and manipulate the tangram pieces into animal forms.

- Stroll through several gardens and compare plants and their characteristics. Ask: Which require low water? Which are bloomers? Contain seed pods?
- Take a tour of the DeGolyer Home and see the hidden room behind the bookcase.
- Create your own map of your favorite garden.

At the Rory Meyer's Children Adventure Garden:

- In the *T. Boone Pickens Pure Energy* area, use mirrors to harness energy to spin the targets.
- In the *Incredible Edible Garden*, talk about corn and the products produced by this natural plant.

Dinosaur Valley State Park

254-897-4588
1629 Park Road 59 Glen Rose, TX
www.tpwd.state.tx.us/state-parks/dinosaur-valley

WHAT: 1,272 acres of park land along the Paluxy River including real dinosaur tracks in the riverbed

HOURS: Park open daily 8am – 10pm for day use only.

ADMISSION: $7/day; 12 & under – Free; Additional fees apply for camping

Identifying and stepping in dinosaur tracks in the rocks along the riverbeds was exciting. The Texas terrain created some challenges to young visitors but it did not stop them. It's fascinating to think this north Texas area actually used to be on the coastline back when the dinosaurs roamed the earth. Luckily for us they left some footprints for us to view thousands of years later.

Inside the visitors center there are two fiberglass models of dinosaur tracks - a 70-foot Apatosaurus and a 45-foot Tyrannosaurus Rex in addition to lots of dinosaur history. Take the time to read the educational information, mentioning interesting tidbits to pre-readers.

The State Park is well maintained with acres for overnight camping. You can't miss the 70-foot fiberglass Brontosaurus and the 45-foot Tyrannosaurus Rex that welcome you to the park. Dinosaur lovers will be thrilled!

TIPS FROM THE AROUND TOWN MOM

- ✓ *Amenities include: Restrooms, gift shop with cold drinks and snacks, and souvenirs.*
- ✓ *The dinosaur tracks are located in the riverbed, so it is advisable to call ahead to check on river conditions. If the river is too high you won't be able to see the tracks.*
- ✓ *Great photo ops with the large dinosaurs out front of the park as well as the real tracks. Bring your camera.*
- ✓ *There is a free app available for Android & Apple phones where visitors can experience real-time tours, at points of interest throughout the Park.*
- ✓ *Climbing on the rocks in the riverbed might be a challenge for younger children. Be sure to wear sturdy shoes/tennis shoes no matter what your age.*

- Texas natural surroundings make a nice walk for this child - some gravel pathways and large fields.
- Hike down to the river bed and explore the water.
- Visit the large replica dinosaurs at the entrance.

- Great hiking paths and gross motor skills activities!
- Pretend you are a dinosaur moving along the path.
- Large rocks make climbing a challenge with the water at the end its reward.
- Talk about large animal tracks seen on the river bottom.

- Lots of climbing and maneuvering around the large boulders, streams, exposed tree roots and tall grasses.
- Discuss dinosaurs; their height, weight and the time period they roamed this earth to make the prints come to life.
- While wading, watch for minnows and shell fossils.
- Talk about rock specimens. Ask: What types of rocks do you see?

- Describe the terrain during the time of the dinosaurs. Ask: What challenges would there be to live at that time?
- Research dinosaur life and diet. Ask: What plants are still left today that may have fed the dinosaurs? What has become extinct?
- Notice the flow of the water along the river. Ask: Where does it come from and where is it going?
- Talk about town development. Ask: Where is the closest town and how is it positioned with respect to the river? Why?

Fort Worth Botanic Gardens

817-871-7673
3220 Botanic Garden Blvd., Fort Worth TX
www.fwbg.org

WHAT: 110 acres of simplicity and perfect harmony.

HOURS FOR THE JAPANESE GARDENS: Monday - Sunday 9am – 7pm (Daylight Savings Time) and 9am – 5pm (Standard Time)

HOURS FOR THE CONSERVATORY: Monday - Saturday 10am – 6pm; Sunday 1pm – 6pm (Daylight Savings Time); Mon – Sat 10am – 4pm; Sun 1pm – 4pm (Standard Time)

HOURS FOR OTHER GARDENS: Open daily dawn - dusk

ADMISSION TO THE JAPANESE GARDENS: $5/Adults; $4.50/Seniors; $3/Children ages 4-12; Children under 3 - Free

ADMISSION TO THE CONSERVATORY: $2/Adults - $1/Seniors and children ages 4-12; Children under 4 - Free

ADMISSION TO OTHER GARDENS: Free

The Fort Worth Botanic Gardens are the oldest botanical gardens in Texas and home to over 2,500 species of native and exotic plants. These gardens are just heaven to stroll through and quite extensive, as they include 23 specialty gardens. Don't try to get finished in a day with little ones. Be prepared to come back another day. After all, it's free!

Gardens include the Rose Garden, the Perennial Garden, the Fragrance Garden, the Four Season Garden and the most popular Japanese Gardens.

Located in the Fort Worth Cultural District, combine this trip with many of the museums in the area.

TIPS FROM THE AROUND TOWN MOM

✓ *Amenities include: Restrooms, water fountains and gift shop*

✓ *Many educational placards with flip tops line the walkways for kids to read and look at the pictures to identify plants and animals.*

✓ *Benches are available along the way to rest.*

- Explore all of these gardens!
- Show the one year-old different plants; their colors, shapes and textures.
- Try out those little feet on the paths and bridges.
- Lining the walkways, press the buttons on the placards to listen and identify various animal sounds such as a turkey, doves, owl and several others.

TWOS & THREES

- The Rose Gardens and Fragrance Gardens make a wonderful sensory discovery.
- Within the Perennial Gardens, pick out different kinds of flowers and other floral plants.
- Find the circular paths and identify the square ones.
- Bring colored tissue paper and make some of the pretty flowers you see.
- Take time to talk to each other through long tubes along the walkways.

FOURS & FIVES

- The Japanese Gardens are most intriguing in this garden area.
- Walk along the paths and cross the little bridges.
- Maneuver in and around these beautiful serene pagodas and shrines.
- Feed the koi carp in the pond for an energetic rustle of activity.
- Visit the Fragrance Garden.

SIX & BEYOND

- Talk about plants and growing seasons, colors and textures and a cultural theme found in the Japanese gardens.
- Look carefully in the Cactus garden. Ask: How are these plants fed and sustained?
- Describe the differences in all the gardens and make a chart to show the diversities.
- At home try to grow a garden or maintain a bonsai tree. Patience is a must.

Grapevine Botanical Gardens

411 Ball Street, Grapevine, TX
www.grapevinetexas.gov/facilities.aspx?page=detail&rid=6

WHAT: Park with trails, streams, ponds, sitting areas and hundreds of varieties of plants for viewing

HOURS: Dawn to dusk, 365 days/year

ADMISSION: Free; Donations accepted

This beautiful park is one of the best kept secrets in the metroplex. It truly took my breath away with its lush natural beauty and tranquil setting. It's the kind of place I'd love to curl up with a book in the shade.

Don't expect it to be the Dallas Arboretum or Fort Worth Botanic Gardens as it is not. Instead, it is much smaller and easier to navigate, a perfect place to introduce your youngster to the natural world. Combine this with the nearby Grapevine Historical District, as the gardens are located near Heritage Park. Walk around the gardens or tour the historical area, then let your child burn off some steam at the adjacent playground.

An educational compost area as well as Butterfly Sanctuary is included in this garden park. A covered pavilion with stone benches used for educational programs is a great place to have a snack or picnic if it's not being used.

TIPS FROM THE AROUND TOWN MOM

- ✓ *Amenities include: Restrooms, water fountains and covered picnic area in the adjoining Heritage Park.*
- ✓ *Wear closed toe shoes or boots if it has just rained. There are many dirt paths in this park.*
- ✓ *Fish food is available for purchase for twenty five cents.*
- ✓ *Mailboxes are scattered throughout the park containing various park information.*
- ✓ *Several areas are identified as "photo op" spots with a bronze camera icon.*

- This is an excellent place for this age group to practice gross motor skills such as running and walking in the wide open spaces.

- Introduce your child to textures including the many large planter vases scattered throughout the gardens. Touch the rough tree trunks and the stone pillars holding up the arbor covered pavilion area.

- Listen to the water fountains and let your child touch the water with their hands or feet in the water overflow part of the fountains.

- At the playground, try out the bucket swings.

- Identify the colors of the flowers.

- Ask: Do the flowers have a scent?

- Count the large trees in an area.

- Point out the letters "e" and "t" in the placards. Identify the letters in the word "earth."

- Go to the bridge in the garden area and view the koi fish. Count the number of orange fish.

- Using paper, do a rubbing on the stone pathways, large planter vases and tree trunks.

- Go to the flower gardens and discuss how the flowers are the same or different. Compare and contrast leaf sizes.

- Count the number of bird feeders in the natural areas.

- At the koi fish pond, ask: Are the koi fish bigger than your hand? Are they bigger than your arm or leg?

- Have fun doing a "Seek and Find." Together, find the following objects located throughout the park: stone crosses, mother holding child sculpture, metal butterflies, waterfall and the dog memorial for a beloved K-9 dog.

- Read the placards and identify the plants shown in the photographs.

- At the creek bank, introduce the concept of erosion and talk about evidence of erosion seen by the exposed tree roots.

- At the Compost Corral, discuss composting and try your hand at the compost tumbler.

- Introduce new vocabulary: *compost, sanctuary, memorial, pavilion, arbor.*

- Discuss the steps necessary to make a botanical garden.

Heard Natural Science Museum & Wildlife Sanctuary

972-562-5566
One Nature Place, McKinney, TX
www.heardmuseum.org

WHAT: 289-acre wildlife sanctuary with 6.5 miles of nature trails and exhibits of Central Texas wildlife

HOURS: Tuesday - Saturday 9am - 5pm; Sunday 1pm - 5pm

ADMISSION: Varies per season – see website.

The Heard Museum, a smaller museum with plenty of outdoor space to explore, is an excellent place to introduce all children, but especially younger ones, to the world of science and nature.

What makes this location unique is its outdoor nature trail and wildlife sanctuary combined with a natural science museum. Outside, visit live animals in the "Animals of the World" exhibit and the native Butterfly Garden (open seasonally). Take a stroll along the nature trails and make a stop at the newly re-located early Texas pioneer buildings in the Educational Village.

Indoors the museum is bursting with natural treasures focusing on Texas, including interactive exhibits of nature and wildlife with several permanent and rotating collections. Pass through the large tree trunk to enter the Living Lab where kids can handle specimens and answer scientific questions.

In addition to their guided nature trails, night hikes and other events, the Heard Museum participates in the spirit of the season with "Halloween at the Heard" and the "Holiday Trail of Lights." Stay tuned to their website or the AroundTownKids calendar: *www.AroundTownKidsMcKinney.com/events.htm*

TIPS FROM THE AROUND TOWN MOM

- ✓ *Amenities include: Restrooms inside, water fountains, gift shop with limited drinks and snacks.*
- ✓ *Nice grassy areas for picnics or on tables in the woods.*
- ✓ *This outing is not conducive for strollers; better for infant to be in a backpack or other carrier.*
- ✓ *A dinosaur dig, or giant sandbox with fossils hidden in the sand, is located in the indoor museum.*
- ✓ *October–February is generally a time when they display the large animatronic dinosaurs along the nature trails. Great for dinosaur lovers!*

Outside:

- Take a walk in the forest and find the sycamore tree.
- Watch for squirrels, birds, little bugs and lizards.
- The path is created with lots of ups and downs. Great for these little legs!

Inside:

- Head to the "Animal Hospital" in the back to play with stuffed animals.
- See the live animals such as snakes, owls, iguana etc.

TWOS & THREES

Outside:

- In the museum entryway, ask: Can you find the frog sculptures?
- Create a treasure hunt looking for acorns, bird feathers, berries and moss.
- At the "Animals of the World" exhibit, find the animal(s) with the striped tail.
- Make some animal sounds.

Inside:

- Ask: Is the sugar glider or flying squirrel hiding? Lift the flap to find them.
- In "Paleo Lab" touch the animal skins for a tactile experience.
- Hunt for fossils in the sandbox.

FOURS & FIVES

Outside:

- Walk the 1 mile nature trail and discover the native Texas terrain.
- Ask: Can you find a source of water?
- At the "Animals of the World" exhibit, notice the deer. Ask: What do deer eat?

Inside:

- In "Texas Treasures," ask: Can you find the buttons and decorative painted seashells?
- In the "Living Lab," view the dioramas. Ask: Can you find a skunk? A snake?
- At the beehive, discuss their activities. Ask: What does a beekeeper wear?

Outside:

- In the museum entry way, look for different indigenous plant species.
- At the creek, ask: What types of life survived here thousands of years ago?
- At the "Animals of the World" exhibit, ask: In which family does the capybara belong?

Inside:

- In the Hall of Geology, ask: How many rocks or minerals can you identify?
- Stop by the mastodon teeth. Ask: What size toothbrush would he need?
- Find the passenger pigeon. Discuss extinction.

Special Interest Exhibits & Museums

Special interest exhibits are created to introduce a personal collection, different occupations, interesting hobbies, or unique interests of those in the community. Often special interest exhibits offer a historic window into the minds of specific groups of people and collections. There are numerous cultural museums in our DFW metroplex and new ones pop up often. Select those that have raised your curiosity and those which offer information on personal hobbies.

Special Interest Exhibits & Museums are places to encounter things you & your children know nothing about or want to broaden your knowledge, to ask questions, find answers, and see in new ways.

Know Where to Go
Suggested Special Interest Exhibits
& Museums in DFW

150 Years of Fort Worth History: Fire Station No. 1 – Fort Worth
www.funmuseum.org

Adrian E. Flatt Hand Exhibit – Dallas
www.juliatexas.com/ historichands.htm

American Museum of the Miniature Arts – Fair Park, Dallas
www.hallofstate.com

Audie Murphy Cotton Museum – Greenville
www.cottonmuseum.com

Botanical Research Institute of Texas – Fort Worth
www.brit.org

Cattle Raisers Museum – Fort Worth
www.cattleraisersmuseum.org

Collin County Farm Museum - McKinney
www.co.collin.tx.org

Cowtown Cattle Maze - Fort Worth
www.cowtowncattlepenmaze.com

Dallas Firefighters Museum – Dallas
www.dallasfiremuseum.com

Dallas Holocaust Museum – Dallas
www.dallasholocaustmuseum.org

Denton County Courthouse-on-the-Square – Denton
www.co.denton.tx.us/dept/hcm.htm

Denton Firefighters' Museum - Denton
www.discoverdenton.com/ pageimages/Fire%20Fighter%20 Museum%202007.pdf

Fan Man – Dallas
www.fanmanusa.com

Fort Worth Museum of Science and History – Fort Worth
www.fwmuseum.org

Fountain Place – Dallas
www.fountainplace.com

Freedman's Cemetery Memorial – Dallas
www.freepages.history.rootsweb. ancestry.com

Hall of State – Fair Park, Dallas
www.hallofstate.com

International Museum of Cultures – Duncanville
www.internationalmuseumofcultures .org

Leonard's Department Store Museum – Fort Worth
www.fwculture.com/leonards_ museum.htm

Mary Kay Museum – Dallas
www.marykaymuseum.com

Morton Museum - Gainesville
www.mortonmuseum.org

National Cowgirl Museum and Hall of Fame – Fort Worth
www.cowgirl.net

National Multicultural Western Heritage Museum and Hall of Fame – Fort Worth
www.cowboysofcolor.org

National Scouting Museum – Irving
www.bsamuseum.org

Pegasus Plaza and Bell Plaza – downtown Dallas
> www.culturenow.org/entry&permalink =14002&seo=AT-T-Plaza_HLM-Design-and-Jarvis-Putty-Jarvis-Architects

Perot Museum of Nature and Science – Dallas
> www.perotmuseum.org

River Legacy Science Center – Arlington
> www.riverlegacy.org

Sci-Tech Discovery Center - Frisco
> www.mindstretchingfun.org

Sixth Floor Museum – Dallas
> www.jfk.org

Stockyards Historic Museum – Fort Worth
> www.stockyardsmuseum.org

Tandy Archaeological Museum – Fort Worth
> www.tandyinstitute.org/aboutthe museum.cfm

Texas Civil War Museum – Fort Worth
> www.texascivilwarmuseum.com

Texas Cowboy Hall of Fame – Fort Worth
> www.texascowboyhalloffame.com

Thanks-Giving Square – Dallas
> www.thanksgiving.org

The Labyrinth – Dallas
> www.labyrinthmetaphysical.com

What Your Kids Can Learn Here
Age Appropriate Activities for Special Interest Exhibits & Museums

ONE YEAR OLDS

- Build strong gross motor skills throughout the location.
- Introduce artifacts by name using simple terms.
- Touch and feel artifacts where allowed and use emotional words to describe how each feels.

TWOS & THREES

- Count items in the exhibits.
- Group specific artifacts into sets of tools or toys.
- Identify colors and shapes.
- Participate in as many hands-on projects and displays as available.

FOURS & FIVES

- If a film is featured, watch some of the presentation.
- Compare similar artifacts with those that have been seen at other locations.
- Draw pictures of favorite or interesting artifacts.
- Look for exhibits of uniforms and costumes and discuss its purpose.
- Role play with hands-on tools and/or costumes that may be available.

SIX & BEYOND

- Talk about how artifacts were created or manufactured.
- Discover special people who may have been featured in the exhibit.
- Define *vintage* and *antique*.
- Identify religious and ceremonial artifacts from aesthetic examples.
- Ask: How does this exhibit make you feel? Compare your thoughts with your child's.
- Ask: How does this exhibit illustrate our culture?
- Visit an associated history museum to enhance the school curriculum.

Special Interest Exhibits & Museums
Featured Destinations

Audie Murphy American Cotton Museum

Fort Worth Museum of Science & History

Fountain Place

Perot Museum of Nature & Science

Stockyards Historic Museum

Audie Murphy American Cotton Museum

903-450-4502
600 Interstate 30 Frontage Rd Greenville, TX
www.cottonmuseum.com

WHAT: A museum depicting the impact of the cotton industry and the historical significance of our military heroes, especially Audie Murphy.

HOURS: Tues - Sat @ 10am - 5pm; Closed Sundays, Mondays and major holidays

ADMISSION: $6/Adults; $4/Seniors; $2/Kids 6 - 18yrs; 5 & under – Free

The Audie Murphy Cotton Museum, formerly known as the Cotton Museum, offers two topics of exhibits: the cotton industry and the life of local war hero, Audie Murphy. Housed inside a barn shaped building, both exhibits are well done.

Cotton played a major role in the livelihoods of many local farmers. This museum has wonderful artifacts, both historic and contemporary, depicting the hard labors of this industry.

In addition to the cotton theme, an extensive collection of donated personal artifacts from Audie Murphy are on display. We learned a lot about this local war hero.

The property houses several other points of interest including a war memorial, confederate memorial and historic home.

TIPS FROM THE AROUND TOWN MOM

✓ *Amenities include: Restrooms and Gift shop with reasonably priced military theme items for sale.*

✓ *There is a battle simulator with the sounds of blasting guns and a moving floor while viewing battle scenes. You know if your child will be scared of this or not.*

- Inside the museum introduce a variety of new vocabulary by calling out names of the artifacts on display.
- Walk the grounds and run through the grasses.
- Point out the fruit hanging from the trees.
- At the war memorial, play peek-a-boo around the statues and trees.

TWOS & THREES

- Identify the variety of colors within Audie Murphy's military medal collection.
- Touch the cotton plants and seeds and describe how it feels.
- Measure your child's size against the large machines that were used in the cotton industry and farming.
- At the war memorial, make a paper-and-crayon rubbing of some of its letters.

FOURS & FIVES

- View Audie Murphy's personal and military effects, weapons, uniforms, 2nd grade report card, etc.
- Talk about the cotton picking process from the informative dioramas depicting life at a cotton mill.
- Try to card some cotton on the hands-on display.
- Peer into the 1915 Low House model.
- Find the vintage gasoline pump, a bonnet, cotton tongs and a fire bucket.

SIX & BEYOND

- Watch the 17 minute video about Audie Murphy. Ask: Who was Audie Murphy and what was his contribution to society?
- Ask: What is a cotton gin and who invented it? Why was this such an important invention?
- From the display, talk about which products come from cotton and cotton seeds.
- Walk into the battle simulator, hear sounds of battle and experience the floor shake as you watch battle scenes.
- At the war memorial, ask: What materials were used to create the sculpture of Audie Murphy and the memorial? Why were these materials chosen?

Fort Worth Museum of Science & History

817-255-9300
1501 Montgomery Street, Fort Worth
www.fwmuseum.org

WHAT: Hands-on exhibits, OMNI Theater, planetarium

HOURS: Mon - Sat @ 10am - 5pm; Sun @ 12pm - 5pm

ADMISSION: $15/Adults; $11/Kids ages 2-11; $13/Seniors; Under 2 - Free
See website for OMNI Theater and planetarium pricing as it varies per show.

There is a lot to see and do here as this is not only the Science and History Museum, but also includes the Forth Worth *Children's Museum*, catering to ages 8 and younger, the OMNI Theater and the planetarium. The *Children's Museum* allows the child to develop a sense of the world around him through hands-on activities. The OMNI Theater and planetarium feature fascinating shows on a variety of topics, some purely entertaining, for all ages. Check their schedule to see what's playing.

The museum has several permanent collections including the ever-popular and interactive *DinoLabs* and *DinoDig* as well as *Energy Blast.* This latter exhibit is geared towards eleven years and older and is filled with many interactive exhibits which tell the dynamic story of energy resources in North Texas. The entrance to the exhibit includes a 4-D movie which younger children will enjoy parts of this adventure such as the water misting. Do visit the permanent exhibits each time you visit. Children often see something new each time they go. Consider having your child participating in one of the museum's educational classes.

Upstairs you will find the *Cattle Raisers Museum,* part of the admission price. The *Cattle Raisers Museum* is a 10,000 square foot exhibition outlining and celebrating the vital history of the cattle industry. Kids can participate in interactive exhibits such as riding a horse and learning to herd cattle using a simulator.

TIPS FROM THE AROUND TOWN MOM
- ✓ *Restrooms, gift shop and snack bar available.*
- ✓ *If you think you'd like to go to the OMNI Theater or planetarium, buy the combo ticket and save some money.*

In the Children's Museum:

- Visit the Children's Museum devoted to infant and 1 year old play with blocks and soft toys.

In the Cattle Raisers Museum:

- Listen to the cattle diorama with figures that "speak."
- Point out sculptures, cowboys, horses, hats, etc.

In the Children's Museum:

- The Children's Museum offers outdoor water play stations, gravity demonstrations, grocery store, hospital and construction activities.
- At water play, ask: What floats? What sinks?
- Play in the grocery store, pretend to go shopping. Count the items you put in the shopping cart. Ask: Do you see things that mommy buys at the store? Separate the foods by color. Put them in the bins by sorting.
- In the hospital have your child pretend to be a doctor, nurse, or the patient.
- Identify the different types of reptiles in the glass cages. Ask: Can you find the turtle or the starfish?

In the Cattle Raisers Museum:

- Name the clothing the cowboy is wearing.
- Introduce new vocabulary: *holster, chaps, vest, boots.*
- Count the number of cows and horses in the displays.
- Point out the shiny saddles.

In the Children's Museum:

- The water play area allows water fun with water guns. Race cars on the tracks and keep track of first, second, and last.

At the DinoDig:

- Point out which dinosaur bones are bigger. Ask: Are dinosaurs still live today?
- Explain what fossils are.
- Point out the large dinosaur footprint fossil and measure its size against your child's.

In the Cattle Raisers Museum:

- The Cattle Raisers Museum allows exploration of the Wild West. Point out the different types of saddles.

- View the spur collection and explain the differences, as well as what they are used for.

- Allow your child to try his hand at the cattle herding simulator, the "Ride Along Round Up."

- Count the number of feathers in the Native American headdress.

- Introduce new vocabulary relating to Cowboy foods: *sourdough bullets, saddle blankets, Pecos strawberries.*

SIX & BEYOND

At the DinoDig:

- Compare dinosaur characteristics to those of present-day creatures.

- Identify the various dinosaurs, using the manipulatives provided.

- Use the imaging station to reconstruct your own dinosaur based on information learned in the exhibit.

- Ask: What is a paleontologist? Talk about the role of the archaeologist in telling history.

- Identify the tools used in digs and determine what they are used for.

In the Cattle Raisers Museum:

- Point out the different types of brands and how they are unique to the individual ranch.

- Try to read the symbols. Ask: What is a longhorn?

- Test your child's knowledge of cow by-products at the glowing steer.

- Explain how a windmill works.

- View the cattle trails from the 1860s to the 1880s using the light up maps.

In the Energy Blast:

- Watch how wind can be used to light up a baseball field in the model.

When your kids' eyes glaze over, the outing is done!

Fountain Place

1445 Ross Ave, Dallas, TX

WHAT: 172 Water falls within lush water pool landscape.

HOURS: Open daily during daylight hours

ADMISSION: Free

Located in downtown Dallas, Fountain Place is a hidden adventure for those of us who don't frequent the area. Designed by acclaimed architectural firm of I.M. Pei & Partners, Dallas is home to this marvel of architectural engineering and water wonderland.

Just behind the Fountain Place building sits a square slate area. This area is designed with holes in the ground forming waterspouts that are activated by a computer-generated pattern. Water may shoot up from the center or edges alone, in wave patterns or just every other hole. And then, just as it began, the water will stop all together. Although this may not be continually monitored, be prepared for officials to request that children not enter the fountains.

These fountains are surrounded by water pools and green plant landscaping. Suggested parking along Ross Avenue.

TIPS FROM THE AROUND TOWN MOM
- ✓ Pack a picnic and do some people watching.
- ✓ Combine this with a trip to nearby Klyde Warren Park for more outdoor fun.

- Listening to water can be soothing and watching the water spring up suddenly can produce wonderful expressions.
- Touch the water and use emotional words to describe its feeling.
- Walk up the steps and around the trees to enhance coordination.

- As the water shoots up, have your child clap his hands in rhythm.
- Introduce the word *pattern* and explain what this word describes. Ask: Can you find other patterns at this location?

- Stimulating sharp memory skills, ask your child to guess the next water sequence.
- Look around this area. Ask: What else do you see here?
- Talk about the trees. Ask: How do they survive here?
- Talk about the other people you see. Ask: What are they doing? Where are they going? How do they feel?
- Walk up the stairs to the street, look both ways. Ask: What do you see?

- Ask: Where does the water come from?
- Talk about how computer generated software designed for this activity.
- Ask: How many sequences are there?
- Discuss what goes on in the Fountain Place building.

Perot Museum of Nature and Science

214-428-5555
2201 N. Field Street, Dallas, TX
www.perotmuseum.org

WHAT: 11 awe-inspiring, interactive science and nature exhibit halls for all ages.

HOURS: Mon - Sat @ 10am - 5pm; Sunday @ Noon - 5pm. See website for seasonal hours.

ADMISSION: $15/Adults; $12/Students & Seniors (65+); $10/Children 2 – 11 yrs; Under 2 - Free

This superbly designed state-of-the-art museum with all the latest high-tech and "green" amenities replaces the Fair Park Dallas Museum of Science and Nature.

The Perot Museum is the collaboration of experts within a variety of higher education disciplines. Their thoughtful attention to details is noticed by every aged participant, including the youngest early readers, as witnessed in the carefully selected vocabulary on display placards. This includes the creation of separate spaces within the same concept which allows a variety of age groups to explore shared concepts of technology, mathematics and science together, yet keeping the boundaries. This was helpful with our group of mixed ages.

Your educational adventure begins even before you enter the museum with the outdoor displays of environmentally-friendly materials, artistic sculpture, and water play as well as displays in the lobby.

Using multiple learning styles including kinesthetic, tactile, visual, and auditory, this location understands that not everyone is intellectually stimulated the same way. The lowest level houses the Children's Area. The levels progress upwards to the highest level designed for advanced learners. In addition to the advanced technology used to create many of the exhibits, you will enjoy the non-computer generated activities requiring hand manipulation (rolling bars, lift boards, and puzzle makers, etc) with little ones.

TIPS FROM THE AROUND TOWN MOM

- ✓ *Amenities include: Restrooms, water fountains, gift shop and café.*
- ✓ *Because of its popularity, it is advisable to purchase your tickets online before you go to ensure entry.*
- ✓ *Visit their website homepage and scroll down all the way to see how far your mouse has travelled in inches, pixels and nanojoules.*

- The Children's Area on the lower level is designed for this age as it offers many kinesthetic and tactile activities throughout this area.
- Practice gross motor skills including walking, reaching, and grabbing.
- Introduce new vocabulary: *smooth, bumpy, rough* as part of tactile experiences.
- Manipulate the large piece puzzles and building blocks.
- Introduce colors, shapes, and simple counting—1, 2, 3.

TWOS & THREES

- Outside, ask: Can you find the fossils? Hear the music? Count the frogs?
- In the Children's Area, observe the animals in cages and talk about sizes, count eyes & legs, and body covering (fur, hair, scales, feathers, etc.)
- Count and compare high and low notes on the Musical Steps.
- In the Gems and Minerals Hall, find the "Grape Jelly Geode." Talk about the colors, sizes and shapes seen in the gems and minerals.
- Throughout the museum, find the movement walls and encourage motion-play for its visual experience.
- On the main floor area, look up and all around. Ask: Can you spot the Dancing Water Molecules mobile and the Malawisaurius dinosaur?

FOURS & FIVES

- In the Children's Area, visit the "Dallas Skyline" playscape and allow kinesthetic development with climbing ladders, steps and ramps. Introduce simple machines and identify the lever, plane, and pulley.
- In the "Sports Run" and "Motion Lab", continue gross motor skills while comparing running speeds to a dinosaur and modern day athlete.
- In the "Texas Blackland Prairie" exhibit, experience visual and auditory samples of native plants and animal sounds. Crawl into the tunnel and feel like a prairie dog!
- Practice reading skills by reading a few information panels aloud.
- Ask: Can you find the earthquake simulator? How long can you "survive" an earthquake tremor?
- From the "Life Then and Now" exhibit, view the dinosaur skeleton from above for a different perspective.

- Ask: What does "environmentally-friendly" mean? Explore how the natural elements of air, sun, and rain affect this "green" building.

- Along the escalator to the 4th floor, identify the downtown Dallas buildings seen along the way.

- Watch for hands-on opportunities to engage in scientific methods in the Being Human Hall's scientific laboratory, and math and engineering in the Engineering & Innovation Hall.

- Ask: Can you find the Nobel Prize? What is a Nobel Prize and why is it awarded? Who won it and for what discovery?

- In the Hall of Birds, special exhibits allow your child to design and save his own bird house for a repeat visit continued study.

When you can't find your child, they've lost interest and have moved on!

Stockyards Historic Museum

817-625-5087
131 E Exchange Avenue, Fort Worth TX
www.stockyardsmuseum.org

WHAT: Display of western culture from 1849 to present.

HOURS: Mon – Sat @ 10am - 5pm. During summer open Sundays @ 1pm – 5pm

ADMISSION: Free; $2 Donation appreciated

Located in the historic Livestock Exchange building, built in 1902, this building is a landmark in the heart of the Fort Worth Stockyards National Historic District. I often thought it was empty, but yes, you can go inside, as it is a museum. The museum offers a peek into the history of Fort Worth and cowboy life. Don't miss the "bad luck" wedding dress, barbed wire display and sewing machine.

After a visit to the Stockyards Historic Museum, stop next door at the Cowtown Coliseum. Inside this unique oval building you can smell the red dirt on the track and remnants of the animals - you know what I mean. Even when not in use it is sort of fun to go and sit inside to imagine all the excitement of live man-to-animal test of strength and power. This large open air coliseum houses rodeos every Friday and Saturday evening and sometimes on a Sunday afternoon, barrel racing can be observed. Look for the annual Bill Pawnee Wild West Show, a highlight among true westerners.

TIPS FROM THE AROUND TOWN MOM
- ✓ *Amenities include: Restrooms, water fountains available*
- ✓ *Photography is allowed in this museum.*

ONE YEAR OLDS

- One year-olds will enjoy maneuvering around the wide walkways and up the steps into and in the museum.
- Talk about the different animals you see.
- Identify colors.

TWOS & THREES

- Identify the stuffed animal heads hanging on the walls.
- Touch the leather saddle and feel the tooling.
- This museum has plenty of opportunities to play "I Spy".
- Count the Native American feathers seen in the headdresses.

FOURS & FIVES

- Ask: Can you find the chair made from horns?
- Compare sizes, shapes, and colors of the projectile point exhibit
- Ask: How was Native American life different from cowboy life?
- Talk about the tools and how they were used. Ask: Do we have modern renditions?
- Introduce vocabulary: *cattle drive, headdress, projectile points, saddle.*

SIX & BEYOND

- Ask: Why was life so hard for early pioneers? How was it fun?
- Talk about the kinds of chores and responsibilities children were given.
- Read the exhibit placard about the Swift and Armour Packing Plants. Ask: Can you describe the attributes of a packing plant?
- Talk about the important role the Chisholm Trail played in Texas history.
- Encourage your child to draw his own cattle drive map.

Transportation Exhibits & Museums

Movement and the fascination with power and speed are the main draws to transportation museums. With the pre-school popularity of Thomas the Tank Engine, Jay Jay the Jet Plane, and older ages' interest in war and military strategies, local museums have wonderful exhibits for these interests. After visiting, try a trip on the DART Light Rail System or city bus.

Transportation Exhibits & Museums are one of the best places to use and discuss action words.

Know Where to Go
Suggested Transportation Exhibits & Museums

American Airlines CR Smith Museum – Fort Worth
www.crsmithmuseum.org

Cavanaugh Flight Museum – Addison
www.cavanaughflightmuseum.com

Cold War Air Museum - Lancaster
www.coldwarairmuseum.org/wiki/index.php?title=Cold_War_Air_Museum&useskin=museum

Founders Plaza – DFW Airport
www.dfwairport.com

Frontiers of Flight Museum – Dallas
www.flightmuseum.com

Grapevine Vintage Railroad - Grapevine
www.grapevinetexasusa.com/grapevine-vintage-railroad/

Hanger 10 – Denton
www.hangar10.org/hangar10/Home.html

Interurban Railway Station Museum - Plano
www.plano.gov/departments/parksandrecreation.org

McKinney Street Trolley Barn – Dallas
www.mata.org/index.shtml

Red River Railroad Museum - Denison
www.redriverrailmuseum.org

Trinity Park Depot (outside the zoo) - Fort Worth
817-336-3328

The Trains of Children's Medical Center – Dallas
www.childrens.com

Union Station – Dallas
www.unionstationdallas.com

Vintage Flying Museum – Fort Worth
www.vintageflyingmuseum.org

What Your Kids Can Learn Here
Age Appropriate Activities for Transportation Exhibits & Museums

ONE YEAR OLDS

- Run along tarmacs and practice other gross motor skills.
- Emulate the sounds of the vehicles' motors or horns.
- Introduce the names of various transportation vehicles.

TWOS & THREES

- Compare the sizes of each vehicle. Ask: Are you taller or shorter?
- Within a collection of vehicles, discover characteristics that are the same and different.
- Look for hands-on opportunities to get inside and role play.
- Count the vehicles on display.
- Talk about colors and shapes.
- Ask: Are these vehicles like the ones we have at home?

FOURS & FIVES

- Climb into engines and other models where available.
- Talk about special uniforms worn to conduct, pilot or drive the vehicle.
- Ask: What were these vehicles used for?
- Ask: What materials were used to manufacture these vehicles?
- Make a model: paper airplane, rain gutter sail boat, pinewood box car, or train, etc.
- Race your vehicles. Ask: Which one goes the fastest and why?

SIX & BEYOND

- Take a trip on an airplane, vintage car, or hot air balloon. Write about your experiences.
- Identify different parts of vehicles and their function.
- Ask: What powers the vehicle?
- Discover specific vehicles which have an interesting history.
- Talk about the assembly-line manufacturing process of these vehicles.
- Ask: What is the difference between a map and a chart? How are these documents important?
- Create a map from your house to your school or grocery store.

Visiting Transportation Exhibits & Museums can help calm the fears of children afraid of flying or going on trains by learning more about them.

Transportation Exhibits & Museums Featured Destinations

American Airlines C.R. Smith Museum

Cavanaugh Flight Museum

Grapevine Vintage Railroad

Interurban Railway Station Museum

Red River Railroad Museum

American Airlines C. R. Smith Museum

817-967-1560
4601 Texas Highway 360 at FAA Road, Fort Worth
www.crsmithmuseum.org

WHAT: Exhibits featuring the history of commercial air travel, particularly as it pertains to American Airlines

HOURS: Tues-Sat @ 9am – 5pm; Closed Sunday and Monday

ADMISSION: $7/Adults; $4/Seniors and Children ages 2-18 yrs; under 2- free

This museum offers some excellent hands-on exhibits along with video presentations to show complex concepts of flight dynamics, air vibrations and flight patterns. Be sure to see the movie, "Spirit of American," about the history of American Airlines and air flight in general. It is shown on a 30-foot screen that gives the illusion of an IMAX theater. Smaller children will enjoy "buckling in" for the "flight."

The highlight of the museum for most children (and even adults!) is the flight simulator used to take off and land a plane. A member of the museum staff will assist each child. Visit the vintage plane, Flagship Knoxville, a rare Douglas DC-3 airliner, and enjoy the closeness of DFW airport with its planes flying, oh, so low.

After your visit, take a trip to DFW airport's observation deck and Founders Plaza and listen to actual pilot-to-control tower communications.

TIPS FROM THE AROUND TOWN MOM

✓ *Amenities include: Restrooms, water fountains and gift shop.*

✓ *Special volunteer assistance is necessary for the simulator. It is recommended to call during operating hours to check availability of the simulator. It is first come, first serve: 817-967-5912*

✓ *This museum hosts rotating exhibits, many geared towards children, so check their website before your trip.*

- Walk through the large exhibit areas and encourage touching.
- Sit with your child on your lap in the mock plane and cockpit and allow reaching for the controls.
- Stroll the area outside, up the small steps, and down the ramped entrance.

TWOS & THREES

- The large vintage Flagship Knoxville plane invites a close look.
- Sit inside the Flagship Knoxville's mock cockpit and the body of the plane and pretend to be a passenger.
- While watching the "IMAX" movie, ask: Do you feel like a pilot?
- Make a crayon rubbing of airplanes using the brass plates provided.
- At the diorama exhibit, push a button and find the light.

FOURS & FIVES

- Watch the 30-foot screen video presentation. Ask: Do you feel like you are flying?
- Walk around the museum and identify as many pieces of airplane artifacts as you can.
- Introduce new vocabulary: *baggage*, *boarding pass*, *uniform*, *pilot*, and *flight attendant*.
- Stop at the large spinning globe in the lobby and point out the continents.

SIX & BEYOND

- Manipulate the displays of air dynamics, air pressure and altitude concepts.
- Take turns in the flight simulator.
- Talk about how the vintage flying costumes have changed to present day uniforms.
- Introduce new vocabulary: *fuselage, rudder, hangar, tail wind, head wind*.
- Identify the mannequin holding the orange sticks up in the air. Ask: What does he do? Learn the meanings of some of their movements.

Cavanaugh Flight Museum

972-380-8800
4572 Claire Chennault, Addison, TX
www.cavanaughflightmuseum.com

WHAT: 50,000 square foot museum of vintage aircraft

HOURS: Mon - Sat @ 9am - 5pm; Sun @ 11am - 5pm

ADMISSION: $10/Adults; $7/Seniors & Military; $8/Children (4-12), $5/Children 3 & under.

Airplane enthusiasts will love this museum as treasures abound. I was very impressed with their extensive collection. There are four large hangars with over 30 planes from WWI, WWII and the Korean War. Surprisingly they even had some old tanks and cars. We enjoyed reading the names on the planes including some funny ones such as, "Bucket of Bolts."

There is also an art gallery with paintings, prints and historical clippings of planes and battles. If you have grandparents who lived around the time of WWII they might enjoy visiting this museum with you.

If you've ever been to Addison's annual July 4th celebration, Kaboom Town, you have seen the "warbirds" flying overhead. They are courtesy of the Cavanaugh Museum.

In 2014 an interactive children's learning area focusing on six aviation subject areas will be added to their campus.

TIPS FROM THE AROUND TOWN MOM

✓ *Amenities include: Restrooms, water fountains, vending machines*

✓ *While the lobby and art gallery are air conditioned, the hangars are not.*

✓ *Museum guided tours are available by appointment*

✓ *If you are a real airplane aficionado, you can buy airplane rides in these vintage planes.*

- Point out the brightly colored animal and cartoon faces on large planes.
- Walk through all four hangars to see the planes.
- Spread your arms and pretend to fly like a plane outside the hangar.
- Emulate the airplane motor sound.

TWOS & THREES

- Count wings, tires, and windows.
- Ask: Can you find the mouse, birds, and faces on the planes?
- Ask: Can you identify the vehicles on display that are not airplanes?
- Climb the observation platform and see a plane from a different perspective.
- Ask: Where is the "nose" of the plane? Where is your nose?

FOURS & FIVES

- Walk to all four hangars and identify the obvious differences in the planes.
- Talk about why some planes are painted with animal faces and others are not.
- Introduce new vocabulary: *pilot, helmet, signal lights, parachute.*
- Let your child make airplane noises and "flap their wings."
- At home: Make a plane from foam board and have an airplane race.

SIX & BEYOND

- Ask: Do planes have different purposes? How can you tell?
- Visit the art gallery, ask: Which paintings look more realistic? Why?
- Ask: Why is the eagle such an important symbol of flight?
- Using your clipboard supplies, draw different parts of a plane.
- Learn about different types of aircraft: jets, helicopters, passenger planes, etc.

Grapevine Vintage Railroad

817-410-8136

Cotton Belt Depot, 707 S. Main St., Grapevine, TX

www.grapevinetexasusa.com/grapevine-vintage-railroad

WHAT: Restored 1896 steam engine & coaches offering old-fashioned train rides

HOURS: See website for hours, many options available.

ADMISSION: One-way, round trip, first class and touring class options available. See website for pricing.

Even if your kids are not "into trains", ride this fun train! We are fortunate to have this operating vintage train in our area for a unique experience. Open or closed passenger cars are available. Either way, you can't escape the sound of the whistle!

Train rides are offered daily with round trips departing Grapevine's Cotton Belt Depot to Fort Worth's Historic Stockyards, and departing Fort Worth's Historic Stockyards to 8th Avenue, Fort Worth and back. For younger children we suggest the latter, the one hour Trinity River ride, or the Grapevine Fun Train. Kids will enjoy crossing the Trinity River and passing by the Fort Worth Zoo.

The Grapevine Fun Train is often combined with seasonal events such as Thomas the Tank Engine and the North Pole Express. Stay tuned to their website or the AroundTownKids.com event calendar: *www.AroundTownKidsFrisco.com/events.htm*

TIPS FROM THE AROUND TOWN MOM

- ✓ *Amenities include: Restrooms and snack bar (cash only) available on board.*
- ✓ *Tickets are not available online for purchase on the day of the trip but a walk up may be available.*
- ✓ *Since the seats are wooden you might consider bringing a small seat cushion for sensitive children who might want to kneel on the seats to look out the window, or just for sitting.*
- ✓ *The train has both open cars and closed cars, but younger children may prefer to ride in the closed cars due to noise and possible soot in the air.*

- With steps to climb, places to run and brick walkways to negotiate, this is a busy place for the one year-old.
- Introduce new vocabulary: *train, tracks, depot*.

- Listen for the train whistle. Ask: Why do trains have whistles?
- Practice making train whistle sounds and the sound of the engine, "chugga chugga."
- Wooden benches make it easy to kneel and see outside the windows.
- Play "I Spy" and identify common objects as you travel along the tracks.
- Let your child hand his/her ticket to the conductor to be punched.

- Using the eyes, follow the tracks to the front of the train as it turns around at the end of the track.
- Encourage conversation with the conductor while he punches your tickets and ask about his uniform.
- Look out the windows and as the train bends around a curve, count how many cars are on the line.
- Introduce new vocabulary: *conductor, engine, rail car*.
- If encouraged by the conductor, make as much noise as you can when you come to a railroad crossing with stopped cars. Ask: What happens?

- Interview the conductor about the history of the Tarantula Train. Ask: When was its first run and where was its destination? What famous man had a hand in its being in Fort Worth? How many runs does this train make in a month?
- Talk about the energy source used by this train. Ask: Is the train powered by coal, electricity or wood? How do you know?
- Ask: Can you feel the weight of the train as it starts down the track?
- Using the map, follow the route this train will take and watch for specific landmarks passing by.
- Treat your child to a beverage while riding and discuss the element of dining on a train.

Interurban Railway Station Museum

972-941-2117
901 East 15th Street, Plano, TX
www.planoconservancy.org

WHAT: Texas Electric Railway Station 1908-1948.

HOURS: Mon - Fri @ 10am - 2pm; Sat @1 - 5pm; Closed Sunday

ADMISSION: Free.

This little train depot is exploding with interesting Texas railroad history. Built by J.R. Strickland in 1908, the Interurban building served as a main stop on the Texas Electric Railway linking Denton to Dallas. The last run was on December 31, 1948.

Along with photographs of trains and stations, children may view documents including tickets and advertising posters. The Texas Electric Railway Post Office Car #360 sits just outside the building. Go inside and see its interior designs. The museum has trained docents to talk with children and make train history fun and exciting.

Consider combining this trip with the Art Center of Plano and picnic at the adjacent Haggard Park. There are plenty of shade trees at the park.

TIPS FROM THE AROUND TOWN MOM

✓ *Amenities include: Restrooms available*

✓ *Year round story time on Fridays @ 10:30am*

- A run in Haggard Park and over the bridge is a must.
- Talk about trains: the wheels, seats, roof and windows.
- Show children Car 360 sitting outside the museum.

Outside:

- Talk about the depot's purpose and the type of vehicle that a depot supports.
- Introduce the concept of people and supplies being transported by train.
- Count the number of mail slots in the 360 car.

Inside:

- Look at the diorama and point out the scene depicted.
- Watch the train circle the track.
- Ring the train's bell.

Outside:

- Take a guided tour of the Car 360 sitting on the tracks.
- Ask: What was this car used to transport?

Inside:

- Look at the photographs of Plano past. Talk about what you see.
- Ask: Why was the railroad important to Plano?
- Ask: How is a mail train different from a passenger train?
- Learn a bit of Morse code or train communications.
- View the mail slots in the train. Ask: What were they used for?

Outside:

- Ask the guide about the building and its structure relating to the depot.
- Discuss what is an "interurban"?

Inside:

- Ask: How did the Interurban get its name and what was its route?
- Learn the difference between a motorman, the ticket agent, line man and railway postal clerk.
- At the diorama, note the fine detail the artist used to depict a country scene along the tracks.
- Trace the route from Denison to Dallas. Ask: How many miles did the Interurban cover? How many stops?
- Ask: Do we still use mail trains today?

Red River Railroad Museum

903-463-5289

101 E. Main Street, Suite 145 Denison, TX

www.redriverrailmuseum.org

WHAT: Railway related artifacts and memorabilia from the Missouri-Kansas-Texas Railroad

HOURS: Thurs – Sat @ 11am – 4pm; Sun @ 1pm – 4pm

ADMISSION: Free, Donations accepted

What makes this museum unique is the fact that it is located in the restored Historic Katy Depot. With so much history in the buildings alone, this is the perfect place to make the bustling days of the railroad come alive for your children.

Jam packed with artifacts and memorabilia from the Missouri-Kansas-Texas Railroad this museum is an unexpected delight for railroad enthusiasts. Train lovers will be pleased to know this museum includes informational films and a train simulator, something I had not seen before and my son was eager to try.

The Katy Depot is the former passenger station, which included a restaurant, pharmacy and barber shop, and general office building of the Missouri-Kansas-Texas Railroad. The depot was the center of operations for the railroad until its merger with the Union Pacific Railroad on August 12, 1988.

TIPS FROM THE AROUND TOWN MOM

- ✓ *Amenities include: Restrooms and items for sale in the museum.*
- ✓ *Because the museum is very full with artifacts, strollers, especially larger ones, might be harder to navigate.*

Inside:

- Point out simple names of objects you see.
- Count aloud to three the objects in sets.

Outside:

- Draw your child's attention to the trains sitting on the tracks.
- Teach her the sound of a train whistle.

Inside:

- Count the number of eyeglasses.
- Introduce new vocabulary: *uniform, overalls.*
- Ask: Can you find the letter "K."
- Walk around the room and count the squares and rectangles.
- Search for red items.

Outside:

- Encourage your child to emulate the sound of the whistle, the chug of the engine, and the conductors call "All Aboard!"
- Ask: What color is this building?

Outside:

- Ask: How are the wheels different on a train versus a car?
- Discuss train whistles and the different pitches of the whistles.
- Ask: What is the purpose of a train whistle?

Inside:

- Measure heights against the conductor mannequin. Ask: Who in the group is taller?
- Find the old train safe and explain what it was used for.
- Introduce new vocabulary: *safe* (as pertains to securing and storing valuable items), *copying press, typewriter, schedule, spittoon.*

Inside:

- Ask: What controls the speed of a train? Do trains have brakes?
- Read a train schedule and identify where the train starts, where it will stop, and how much time does it take.
- At the train office exhibit, identify some of the equipment and compare to contemporary tools performing the same tasks.
- Sit in the train simulator and play engineer.
- Notice the old style of luggage and explain the use of trunks before suitcases.

Outside:

- Ask: What are the differences between a train and a car?
- Discuss the different types of rail cars and what they were used for – example – passenger cars, dining cars, cargo cars, refrigerated cars, flat cars etc.

DFW Area Festivals

Festival List — Know When to Go

Know when best to enjoy Dallas/Fort Worth throughout the year with this handy list of festivals by month.

PLEASE NOTE: "Free" is for admission only. This does not include any fees for parking, concessions or extras.

Festival	City	FREE Admission – Y/N
JAN		
Carrollton MLK Day Parade	Carrollton	Y
Elite News MLK Parade and Festival	Dallas	Y
Fort Worth MLK Day Parade	Ft Worth	Y
Garland Annual MLK Day Parade	Garland	Y
FEB		
Krewe of Barkus	McKinney	Y
MARCH		
Arts in the Square	Frisco	Y
Cowtown Goes Green	Ft Worth	Y
Dallas Blooms	Dallas	N
Festival de los Mavs	Dallas	Y
Noth Texas Irish Festival	Dallas	N
St Patrick's Day Parade	Dallas	Y
Texas Pinball Festival	Dallas	N
Texas Storytelling Festival	Denton	Y
APRIL		
Chocolate Fest	Grapevine	N
Dallas Blooms	Dallas	N
Dallas International Guitar Festival	Dallas	N
Denton Arts & Jazz Festival	Denton	Y
Denton Redbud Festival	Denton	Y
Ennis Bluebonnet Trails Festival	Ennis	Y

Fort Worth Main Street Arts Festival	Ft Worth	Y
Japanese Garden Festival	Ft Worth	N
River Legacy Cardboard Boat Regatta	Arlington	N
Scarborough Faire Renaissance Festival	Waxahachie	N
Southlake Art in the Square	Southlake	Y
Tandy Hills Prairie Fest	Ft Worth	Y

MAY

Annual Butterfly Festival	Plano	N
Asian American Heritage Festival	Plano	Y
Asian Festival	Dallas	Y
Celina Cinqo de Mayo	Celina	Y
CityArts Festival	Dallas	Y
Cottonwood Art Festival	Richardson	Y
Dallas Cinqo de Mayo Festival & Parade	Dallas	Y
Dallas International Festival	Dallas	Y
Dragon Boat, Kite and Lantern Festival	Irving	Y
Japanese Maple Festival	Dallas	Y
Liberty Fest	Farmer's Branch	Y
Main Street Days	Grapevine	N
Mayfest	Ft Worth	N
National Polka Festival	Ennis	N
Scarborough Faire Renaissance Festival	Waxahachie	N
Scottish Festival & Highland Games	Arlington	N
Taste of Addison	Addison	N
Watters Creek Fine Arts Festival	Allen	Y
Wildflower Arts & Music Festival	Richardson	N

JUNE

Allen USA Celebration	Allen	Y
Dog Days of Denton	Denton	Y
Shakespeare in the Park	Dallas	N
Summer Cut: The Happy Funtime Fest	Dallas	N

JULY

4th Fest	Bedford	Y
4th of July Stockyards Style	Ft Worth	Y

Castle Hills Freedom Fest	Carrollton	Y
Celebrate Freedom - Christian Festival	Parker	Y
Fair Park Fourth	Dallas	Y
Farmers Branch Independence Day Celebration	Farmers Branch	Y
Flower Mound Independence Fest	Flower Mound	Y
Fort Worth's 4th	Ft Worth	Y
Freedom Fest	Frisco	Y
Grand Prairie Lone Stars and Stripes Fireworks Celebration	Grand Prairie	Y
Irving Firecracker Fourth	Irving	Y
Kaboom Town	Addison	Y
Little Elm July Jubilee Celebration	Little Elm	Y
Old Fashioned Fourth	Carrollton	Y
Parker County Peach Festival	Weatherford	N
Red, White & Boom	McKinney	Y
Red, White & Lewisville	Lewisville	Y
Richardson Family Fourth Celebration	Richardson	Y
Shakespeare in the Park	Dallas	N
Taste of Dallas	Dallas	N
The Colony Liberty by the Lake Concert	The Colony	Y

AUG

Lion's Club Balloon Festival and Fair	Highland Village	Y

SEPT

Addison Oktoberfest	Addison	N
Bedford Blues & BBQ Fest	Bedford	N
Butterflys & Bugs TX Discovery Gardens	Dallas	N
Grapefest	Grapevine	N
Greek Festival of Dallas	Dallas	N
Kiwanis Butterfly Festival	Southlake	N
McKinney Oktoberfest	McKinney	Y
Plano Balloon Festival	Plano	N
Southlake Oktoberfest	Southlake	Y
State Fair of Texas	Dallas	N
The Fort Worth Music Festival	Ft Worth	N

OCT

Autumn Days Festival	Ennis	Y
Bloomin' Bluegrass Festival and Chili Cookoff	Farmer's Branch	Y
Buttefly Flutterby	Grapevine	Y
Celina Balloon Festival	Celina	N
Cottonwood Art Festival	Richardson	Y
Fiesta Latinoamericana	Dallas	Y
Latino Cultural Center DÍa De Los Muertos	Dallas	Y
Lone Star Storytelling Festival	Frisco	N
Peanut Festival	Whitesboro	Y
Plano International Festival	Plano	Y
Santa Fe Days on the Square	Carrollton	Y
State Fair of Texas	Dallas	N
Worldfest	Addison	N

NOV

Dia De Los Muertos	Ft Worth	Y
Dickens of a Christmas	McKinney	Y
Fort Worth Greek Festival	Ft Worth	Y
Thanksgiving in the Ft Worth Stockyards	Ft Worth	Y

DEC

Candlelight at Dallas Heritage Village	Dallas	N
Carrollton Old Fashioned Christmas	Carrollton	Y
Christmas in the Ft Worth Stockyards	Ft Worth	Y
Christmas on Main Street	Grapevine	Y
Dallas City Lights	Dallas	Y
Dickens in Historic Downtown Plano	Plano	Y
Grapevine Carol of Lights	Grapevine	Y
Holiday at the Arboretum	Dallas	N
Illumination Celebration at the Galleria	Dallas	Y
Kwanzaa Fest	Dallas	Y
Merry Main Street	Frisco	Y
Prosper Country Christmas	Prosper	Y
Santa's Village	Richardson	Y
Six Flags Holiday in the Park	Arlington	N
Vitruvian Lights: Magical Nights of Lights Festival	Addison	Y

Dollar Rating Guide

Dollar Rating Guide — Know Before You Go

Know how much money you'll have to spend on admission prices before you go.

PLEASE NOTE: Activity location price ratings are ranked by adult admission price only and do not factor in parking or any additional fees you may spend during your outings. Prices may be subject to change, so check the destination's website before making plans.

 KEY $ = $1-$9 $$ = $10-$15 $$$ = $16+

FREE

Location Name	Admission Price
Adrian E. Flatt Hand Exhibit	Free
African American Museum-Dallas	Free
African American Museum-Denton	Free
Allen Heritage Center & Museum	Free
American Museum of the Miniature Arts	Free
Amon Carter Museum	Free
Arbor Hills Nature Preserve	Free
A.W. Perry Homestead Museum	Free
Bass Pro Outdoor World	Free
Bayless-Selby House	Free
Botanical Research Institute of Texas	Free
Cabela's	Free
Cedar Ridge Preserve	Free; Donations accepted
Celestial Park	Free
Central Park	Free
Chestnut Square Historical Village	Recommended Donations-$5/Adults, $3/children
Children's Medical Center	Free
Cold War Air Museum	Free
Collin Street Bakery	Free
Coppell Farmers Market	Free
Crape Myrtle Trails	Free
Crow Collection of Asian Art	Free-Suggested donation is $7 for adults and $5 for seniors.
Dallas Center of Contemporary Arts	Free
Dallas Farmers Market	Free
Dallas Museum of Art	Free

McDonald's . . . . Free

McKinney Farmers Market . . . . Free

McKinney Street Trolley Barn . . . . Free

Medical Center of Plano . . . . Free

Mozzarella Cheese Company . . . . Free

Museum of Geometric & MADI Art . . . . Free

Mustangs of Las Colinas . . . . Free

Nash Farm . . . . Free

Old City Cemetery . . . . Free

Pape's Pecan Company . . . . Free

Pegasus Plaza and Bell Plaza . . . . Free

Pioneer Plaza . . . . Free

Plano Farmers Market . . . . Free

Red River Railroad Museum . . . . Free

Reverchon Park . . . . Free

River Legacy Park . . . . Free

River Legacy Science Center . . . . Free

Rockwall County Historical Foundation Museum . . . . Free

SAS Shoe Factory and General Store . . . . Free

Shawnee Trail . . . . Free

Sid Richardson Collection of Western Art . . . . Free

South Dallas Cultural Center . . . . Free

Southwest Dairy Museum . . . . Free

Spring Creek Nature Park . . . . Free

Stockyards Historic Museum . . . . $2 Donation appreciated

Sun Creek . . . . Free

Tandy Archaeological Museum . . . . .Free

Texas Sculpture Garden . . . . Free

Thanks-Giving Square . . . . Free

The Labyrinth . . . . Free

The Trains of Children's Medical Ctr . . . . Free

Union Station . . . . Free

US Bureau of Engraving & Printing Western Currency Facility . . . . Free

UT Southwestern Medical Center . . . . Free

Vetro Art . . . . Free

White Rock Lake Museum . . . . Free

Wimberley Glass Works . . . . Free

$

Location Name	Admission Price
American Airlines C.R. Smith Museum	$4/Adults; $2/Children ages 2-18 yrs; under free; $2/Seniors 55+
American Airlines Center-tours	$5/Adults; $3/Seniors & Children 3-17yrs
Arlington Museum of Art	$2/Adults; $1/Seniors/students
Audie Murphy Cotton Museum	$6/Adults; $4/seniors; $2/Children 6-18 yrs; Free-children 5 and under
Blue Bell Ice Cream Factory Tour	$5/Adults; $3/Kids 6-14 yrs
Cedar Hill State Park	$7/Adults; Children 12 Years and Under-Free
Collin County Farm Museum	$3/Adults & Seniors; $2/Youth (6-16); Children under 6 years-Free
Cowtown Cattle Maze	$6/Person
Dallas Children's Aquarium	$8/Adults; $6/Children (3-11) & seniors (65+); Ages 2 & under–Free
Dallas Firefighters Museum	$4/Adults; $2/Children
Dallas Heritage Village	$7/Adult; $5/Senior (65+); $4/Child (4 to 12 years)
Dallas Holocaust Museum	$8/Adults; $6/Ages 6-18 yrs & Seniors
Dinosaur Valley	$7/day; 12 & under-Free
Eisenhower Birth Place	$4/Adults; $3/Ages 6-18; 5 and under-Free
Fielder House Museum	$3/Person
Frank Buck Zoo	$4/Children ages 1-12yrs; $5/Senior Citizen & Military; $6/Ages 13 yrs +
Frisco Heritage Museum	$4/Adults; $2/Kids 5-11 yrs; 4 & under-Free; $8/Family
Frontiers of Flight Museum	$8/Adults; $6/Seniors ; $5/ Ages 3-17; Children under 3 FREE
Ft Worth Nature Center and Refuge	$5/Adults; $2/Ages 3-17 yrs; under 3 free; $3/Seniors
Heard Craig Historical Center	$5/Adults; $3/Children
Heritage Farmstead Museum	$2/person; 4 & under are free
International Museum of Cultures	$5/Adults; $4/Seniors & Children; 3 yrs & under -Free
Knapp Heritage Park	$3/person
Log Cabin Village	$3.50/Adults; $3/3-17 yrs; under 3-free
Morton Museum	Free
Mrs. Baird's Bakery	Free
National Multicultural Western Heritage Museum & Hall of Fame	$6/adults; $4/seniors; $3/students; Free-children 5 and under
National Scouting Museum	$8/Adults; $6/Seniors & Children 4-12; $5/Scouts/Scouters; Free-Children under 4
Nokona Athletic Goods Company	$5/Adult; Free for students with ID
Old Red Museum of Dallas County	$8/adults; $6/seniors; $5/kids 3-16 yrs
Owens Spring Creek Farms	$5/person; children under 2 - FREE - SEASONAL
Penn Farms Agricultural History Center	$/Adult; Children 12 yrs and under-Free
Sci-Tech Discovery Center	$7/Person; $5.50/Seniors; Under two-Free
Texas Civil War Museum	$6/Adults; $3/Ages 7-12; Children 6 and under-Free with adult
Texas Cowboy Hall of Fame	$5/Adults; $3/Kids 5-12yrs; 4 and under are free
Texas Discovery Gardens	$8/adults; $6/ages 60+; $4/ages 3 to 11; Under 3 yrs-Free;
Texas Freshwater Fishery Center	$5.50/Adults; $4.50/Seniors; $3.50/Ages 4-12

Texas Motor Speedway . . . . $8/Adults; $6/Seniors & Children 12 & under

Vintage Flying Museum . . . . $8/Adults; $5/Ages 13-17 & Seniors; $3/Ages 6-12; Kids under 6-Free

$$

Location Name	Admission Price
Ball-Eddleman-McFarland House	$15/Adults; $7.50/Children
Cattle Raisers Museum	$14/Adults; $10/Kids ages 2-12 yrs & Seniors
Cavanaugh Flight Museum	$10/Adults; $7/Seniors & Military; $5/Ages 4-12; Children 3 & Under: Free
Dallas Arboretum and Botanical Gardens	$15/Adults; $12/Seniors; $10/Ages 3-12; Under 3 yrs-Free
Dallas Zoo	$12/adults; $9/Ages 3-11 yrs & Seniors; 2 & under-Free
Ft Worth Museum of Science and History	$15/Adults; $11/Ages 2-11 yrs; $13/Seniors
Ft. Worth Zoo	$12/Adults; $9/Ages 3-12 yrs & Seniors; Free-2 & Under
Heard Natural Science Museum & Wildlife Sanctuary	Prices vary per season; $9-$11/Adults, $6-$8/Kids
In-Sync Exotics Wildlife Rescue	$10/Adults; $7/Ages 4-12 yrs; under 4-Free
Meadows Museum	$10/Adults; $8/Seniors; Free-children under 12
Modern Art Museum of Ft Worth	$10/Adults; Free for kids 12-under
Museum of Biblical Arts	$12/Adults; $10/Seniors & Students
Nasher Sculpture Center	$10/Adults; Kids 12 & under are Free
National Cowgirl Museum	$10/Adults; $8/Ages 3-12yrs & seniors; 2 & under-Free
Perot Museum	$15/Adults; $12/Students & Seniors; $10/Children; Under 2-Free
Sharkarosa Wilflife Ranch	$10/Adults; $8/Children; Children 2 & under-Free; $8/Seniors
Stockyards Championship Rodeo	$10-$20
Texas Rangers Ballpark Tours	$14/Adults; $11/Seniors; $7/Kids 4-18yrs; Under 4-Free
Thistle Hill	$15/Adults; $7.50/Children

$$$

Location Name	Admission Price
Cowboy Stadium	$17.50/Adults; $14.50/Kids & Seniors
Dallas World Aquarium	$20.95/Adults; $12.95/Ages 3-12 yrs; $16.95/Seniors; Children 2 & under-Free
Fossil Rim Wildlife Center	Weekday: $20.95/Adults; $14.95/Children 3-11, 2 Under Free -more on weekends
Grapevine Vintage Railroad	varies from $10-$28/Adults; $6-$18/Kids
Mesquite Championship Rodeo	$24 and $30/Adults w/ Kids half price; $12/corral seats
SeaLife Aquarium	$19/Adults; $15/Ages 3-12
Sixth Floor Museum	$16/Adults; $14/Seniors; $13/Ages 6-18 yrs; 5 & under-Free

As an additional resource to Kidding Around Town, AroundTownKids.com can be used to further locate places to visit in the Dallas Fort Worth area.

Alphabetical Index

What is AroundTownKids.com?

- Kids Event Calendar for Dallas Fort Worth

- Online Parent Resource Guide — business directory listings for places to go, summer camps, birthday parties, childcare and more

- Coupon Page

- Blog with informative parenting articles, crafts and recipes

On the AroundTownKids website, simply click the "Things to Do" button on the orange menu bar for a selection of places to visit in Dallas Fort Worth by category – everything from local parks, to museums to zoos and a whole lot more.

Before you go on your outing, be sure to click the red "Coupon" tab above the orange menu bar for a variety of coupons from local businesses.

www.AroundTownKids.com

Find Information Quickly with our App!

Using the AroundTownKids iphone app, parents can quickly discover places to go in the DFW metroplex.

How to find us? Scan the QR code to the left, or look us up in the App store by checking the **Lifestyle** Category or typing in **AroundTownKids** in the search bar.

The App is formatted for iPhone, iPad and iPod.

For more information on the AroundTownKids app, visit:
http://www.AroundTownKidsFrisco.com/DFWThingsToDoApp.htm